S0-FBL-623

WITHDRAWN

LET'S TALK
BUSINESS

Improving
Communication
Skills

WITHDRAWN

LET'S TALK BUSINESS

Improving Communication Skills

TOURO COLLEGE LIBRARY
Kew Gardens Hills

Carl L. Kell
WESTERN KENTUCKY UNIVERSITY

Paul R. Corts
OKLAHOMA BAPTIST UNIVERSITY

LITTLE, BROWN AND COMPANY
Boston   Toronto

Kaw Order Wills

Library of Congress Cataloging in Publication Data

Kell, Carl L.
  Let's talk business.

  Includes bibliographies and index.
  1. Communication in management.   I. Corts,
Paul R.   II. Title.
HF5718.K44   658.4′5   81–16465
ISBN 0–316–48646–9   AACR2

Copyright © 1983 by Carl L. Kell and Paul R. Corts

All rights reserved. No part of this book may be reproduced in any form
or by any electronic or mechanical means including information storage
and retrieval systems without permission in writing from the publisher,
except by a reviewer who may quote brief passages in a review.

Library of Congress Catalog Card Number 81–16465

ISBN 0-316-48646-9

9 8 7 6 5 4 3 2 1

MV

Published simultaneously in Canada
by Little, Brown & Company (Canada) Limited

Printed in the United States of America

12/27/00

To Kenneth, Daniel, and Susan Corts
—P.R.C.

To Mother and Dad—who taught me to
"give a good day's work"
—C.L.K.

PREFACE

Let's Talk Business was selected as the title for this book during a pleasant spring afternoon run. We liked it because it speaks to us on several levels. First, it is a familiar greeting between people in a social or business setting. Next, it pinpoints the substance of this book—we are about the business of talking all the time, in business and in private, with a specific interest in personal rewards. Finally, *Let's Talk Business* is a proper label for a fundamental study of human communication in business as opposed to an advanced study of the communication dimension of organizations.

The graphics of *Let's Talk Business* speak for themselves. We believe that a successful businessperson must understand communication theory and communication skills and have the sensitivity to mesh these gears as the communication environment demands. At the beginning of each chapter, we have arranged the gears motif to show relationships where they exist. Within each chapter we have suggested how theory and skill mix and the levels of competence available in that mixture.

If at various times throughout the course of study you can *see* and *feel* those gears operating smoothly, then we will have done our part. If we can help you see where the gears *don't* mesh, where there is sand in the gears causing them to grind, then we will have done our part there as well. For we must come to understand the full range of successes and failures in business communication as part of the enterprise. *Let's Talk Business* is not a doctor's prescription for our communication ills. We do our best work, as does your instructor, as an advisor, not a faith healer. It is with these limits in mind that we humbly offer you our wares.

This book has been designed to provide the widest possible range of communication competence in business. We will present, discuss, and suggest ways and means to learn the basic spoken and written communication skills required by a variety of business and industrial organizations. We have canvassed the available literature on the communication skills needed for entry level employees in business and have prepared the chapters of *Let's Talk Business* based on those data. We are persuaded, as we think you will be, that the most efficient policy in teaching and learning the fundamentals of business communication is to find out what the "real" world wants and then address those issues in appropriate learning experiences.

Let's Talk Business is not concerned with the more popular area of organizational communication. The texts and courses associated with this field deal with the inner workings of modern organizations from a communications perspective. We believe that our text and its development are more properly a part of what we have termed *business communication.* This term encompasses the communication skills necessary for effective daily interaction in business. In a sequence of courses on organizational communication, our text is for a first course in a program of study leading to an undergraduate major or minor in the field. Thus, we will not be as detailed in our discussions of business theory as would be expected of an advanced book in organizational communication.

Let's Talk Business is divided into two parts. Part I is a three-chapter discussion of communication processes, responsibilities, and competences in American business. First, we present an analysis of the typical American business organization, its patterns, and its communication processes, as an introduction to the usefulness of studying business communication. Second, we identify basic mid-management and management positions traditionally found in modern business organizations and the types and forms of communication commonly used in these positions. We stress the importance of communication for business leaders, including government requirements for understandable communication with employees and clients, along with the social responsibility for good communication on the part of business leaders. Third, we have developed a far-reaching set of competences from the literature so that you can see for yourself what you must learn.

Part II is a series of eight chapters that "shows and tells" you how to get a handle on the various skills and how to move toward a measure of competence in those skills—interviewing, writing and editing of written messages, diagnosing and managing communication problems, leadership and group conference skills, public communication, and, through all these areas, effective listening. Throughout these chapters, we are concerned with helping you to be sensitive to the development and use of the appropriate communication skills, written or spoken, in a given situation.

There is sufficient evidence to suggest that employers have vague and incorrect notions about what you have learned to do by majoring or minoring in speech or communication. We hope *Let's Talk Business* will narrow the gap between what business expects you to know and do with your communication skills, and how you can be prepared to meet its demands.

There is little disagreement, however, about what American businesses expect from you in basic communication skills. We are going to talk about those priorities and provide suggestions and advice to get you from where you are now to a point where *you know what you know* and, with that knowledge, can control your communication interaction competently.

Now, let's talk business!

CONTENTS

PART I

UNDERSTANDING BUSINESS COMMUNICATION

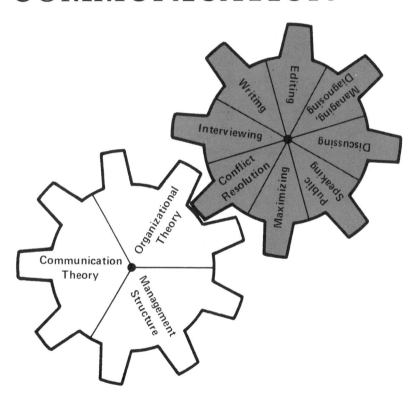

Chapter 1

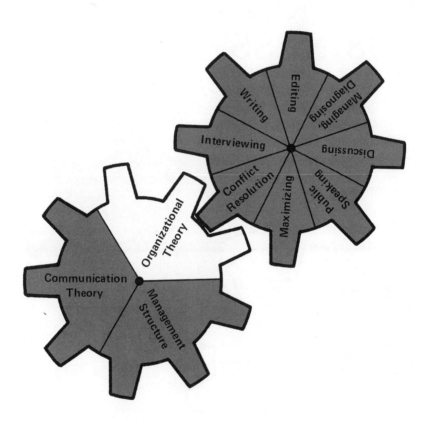

COMMUNICATION PROCESSES IN BUSINESS

This chapter will provide you with the following:

1. an understanding of the formal network structure of American business

2. an understanding of why the formal network came into being

3. an understanding of the basic facts of business communication

4. an understanding of the nature of informal channels (the "grapevine")

5. an understanding of the *process* nature of communication—that is, communication as a personal transaction and a transactional *process*

6. an understanding of the flow of messages (task and human) in downward and upward communication

7. the ability to list and explain the keys to communication effectiveness in business

8. the realization that communication is the central function of organizational behavior

As you begin your study of business communication, you will discover that it is much too early to know what is in store for you or what exciting futures it holds. There are some certainties, however, including death, taxes, and the growth of American business. Our society is certainly becoming more complex, more populous, and more demanding in its needs for services—public, local, state, federal, and *personal*. It is in this last category, personal services, that we find the energy to infuse life into our relationships and to group together in the organizations that *create* social institutions, families, and modern businesses.

Futurists tell us that the last twenty years of this century will see a demand for and a subsequent rise in the number of jobs and careers involving personal services and personal contacts between business and consumer. We have passed through the first wave of the "me" years—a period in which people have affirmed their right to know, to see, to feel, and to express themselves to the fullest, and to expect a good product for a fair price—and we are just beginning to be able to deal personally with the business world as consumers with acknowledged rights and privileges.

The American public is expecting a fair shake from American business, as the rise and maturation of the consumer movement indicates. It is fair to ask, then, just how much the millions of people who work for our businesses and industries expect from their employers. We have seen and will continue to see a dark side of employee-employer relationships—strikes, walkouts, fights, and even work-related deaths. To be sure, we can expect to have these problems so long as there are people working for other people, but, obviously, the majority of business and industrial concerns in our country do not foster such negative conditions for their workers. Modern business has great potential for success or failure, depending on the personal energies and skills of the people involved as they work with one another and as they serve their publics. In short, you can experience a sense of personal growth as you learn to deal with the systems of communication of the business world.

With these views in mind, we will discuss the organizational patterns of American business and the types of communication processes that are operative in these organizations.

COMMUNICATION: THE NETWORK OF AMERICAN BUSINESS

As we have noted, we live in an age of organizations. Within the structures of modern organizations a variety of messages must flow to sustain those organizations. The most recognized channels of communication in modern business are the *formal* and the *informal* patterns. We will discuss each in turn.

Formal organizational structures

As Thayer (1968) argues, the *development* of the formal network within most organizations is the result of communication itself. Written and spoken communications are the instruments by which businesses of all types translate their raw data into information and, in turn, use that information to relate each component of the organization to the others. Harris and Cronen (1979) suggest that an organization and its internal and external communications cannot be understood in isolation. If you want to know about an organization, you must study its communications.

How, then, did the formal pattern of organization come into being, and what does the system look like? We contend that the formal pattern of business communication came into existence to establish and to preserve certain norms:

1. the *control, power,* and *responsibilities* for obtaining the major *goals* of the business, such as sales, consumer services, and so on
2. the subsequent *rights* to divide the work, to limit the patterns of interaction, to coordinate, and to monitor the internal energies of the staff so as to respond effectively to any problem that harms the flow of work
3. the understanding and use of the informal patterns of communication so as to monitor the feedback on and about the organization

Leonard Freed/Magnum Photos, Inc.

Formal network/pattern of business communication

These norms of collective behavior describe the "who we are and what we are expected to do" that guides most communication behavior in the organization.

The structural arrangement of government, organizations, and businesses usually follows similar constructions, ranks, levels, and tiers of workers. As an example, Figure 1.1 is an organizational chart of the communication staff of Executive Vice-President Robert Hartmann, senior officer of the hypothetical Tram Company, a railroad management firm. The chart is typical of those available in the literature.

The following facts of business communication are common to all similarly based charts:

1. The authority, power, esteem, and prestige of the upper levels of management spell out the *goals* of the organization.

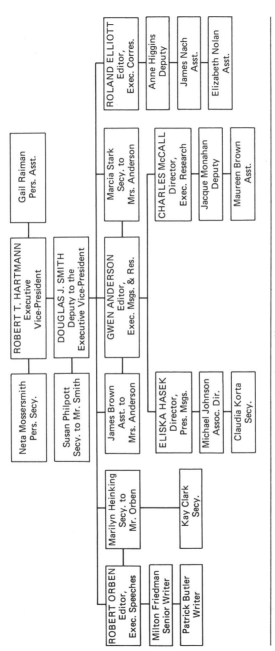

FIGURE 1.1   Organizational chart of communication staff

In Figure 1.1, Mr. Hartmann's roles as the person responsible for the public communication of Tram Company are delegated to Mr. Orben (speeches), Mrs. Anderson (written messages), and Mr. Elliott (written correspondence).

2. The formal structure exists to divide the work load, to limit patterns of structural interaction so that jobs can remain free of structural entanglements, and to set up substructural patterns of interaction so that workers at various levels (horizontal or vertical) can do their jobs.

3. *Downward* communication through the superstructure of the organization is concerned primarily with instructing, with building and maintaining morale, and with moving routine work smoothly.

4. *Upward* communication through the superstructure of the organization is concerned mainly with seeking information for decision making and with reporting on the progress of projects, sales campaigns, internal controls, and so on.

5. Communication that moves up the channel, across status levels, from the bottom to the top, or diagonally is moderately to seriously inhibited by the structure.

6. The formal pattern can reach only a certain level of success and no more. The ability of the network—or any of its parts—to reach a goal is much more limited than that of an informal network of more powerful people who can solve a problem directly. Informal patterns and other configurations are often more powerful than an organization's formal structure.

7. Finally, the power of the formal network is best realized when it delivers information that is accurate, relevant, and, especially, timely.

Informal networks

A loosely arranged network of social interaction in an organization, known as the grapevine, usually forms the most accurate and yet the most suspect avenue of business communication. The grapevine is a natural part of any organization, spreading information across the formal links of the system in various patterns.

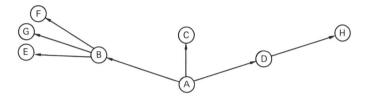

FIGURE 1.2   Typical grapevine pattern

For example, one person may tell three or four members of the organization a piece of news or a rumor. Usually, only one or two members of the original reception network pass along the information. The grapevine network then reaches out to new receivers in what might be called a cluster pattern. Figure 1.2 illustrates the pattern most often discovered in grapevine research.

Obviously, some receiving members will halt the news or rumor, while others will pass it along to a range of people as narrow as their own work place or as wide as the top or bottom of the formal network. Most grapevines are fast—much faster in channel capacity and timeliness than formal systems. Grapevines are also accurate (some suggest as high as 80 percent accuracy), but they seldom carry the whole story with a high degree of fairness to all parties involved.

On the positive side, grapevines are often the best source of feedback about matters that affect the business or organization. We advise that, once you are part of a system, you accept the existence of the grapevine, respect it, listen to it, respond to it, and, at strategic times, feed it. The grapevine is the best social system devised by employees to meet their real needs, their imagined needs, and their fantasies. The grapevine is not to be taken lightly; it can be either an ally or an enemy. Often, a manager or supervisor will use certain carriers of information within the organization to assure, to explain, to lend credibility to the company, or to support the decisions of top management that affect the entire system. Coupled with the formal channels, the grapevine can control rampant rumors of employee hiring or firing, company expansion, plant shutdowns, and the like. The total success of information transfer and employee acceptance often comes from a skillful use of both networks. In Chapter 8, we will discuss at some length the diagnosis and management of grapevine and related communication problems.

THE PROCESS OF COMMUNICATION

We have defined business communication as the flow of messages within the business environment. In terms of the formal and informal networks of a business, a message is information to which receivers attach meaning—informative or persuasive—depending on their role in the process. We call communication a *process* because it involves ongoing receiving and sending of messages.

The process of communication can be viewed from two perspectives:

1. Communication is a *personal transaction.* Each of us is unique. We see and respond to the world around us in especially personal ways. Because each of us is different, we interpret and act upon messages in ways that are ours alone, unlike anyone else's.
2. Communication is a *transactional process.* We send and receive messages through a variety of channels until the messages have been played out. Communications of all kinds in business and industry (and personal communications as well) must always confront the inherent problem of distortion to some degree.

CLASSIFICATION OF MESSAGES

In organizations and businesses, messages are carried primarily through oral or written communication channels. Most messages can be classified as either *task* messages (services, reports, control, maintenance, inventory, and so on) or *human* messages (routine concerns about morale and productivity).

Downward communication from supervisors or managers to their subordinates usually involves the following task messages:

1. *job instructions,* through a combination of written material and show-and-tell

2. information concerning company *rules, procedures,* and *goals* that require the subordinate's full attention on the job
3. *feedback* concerning the subordinate's work—an important response to "How Am I Doing?" (Allen, 1977)

Upward communication involves messages that flow up the channels to provide feedback, to make suggestions, or to report on the progress of daily or regularized assignments. Typical written upward communication messages include:

1. sales and purchase orders
2. inventory completion and controls
3. cost records
4. work-in-progress reports
5. shipping and receiving orders
6. production and maintenance records

Typical oral upward communication messages include:

1. formal and informal performance appraisal interviews
2. telephone conversations
3. complaints, creative ideas, or arguments that need airing to increase the organization's strength and to improve its performance

KEYS TO COMMUNICATION EFFECTIVENESS

Employees in any business soon develop a keen sense for successful upward communications and an abundant faith in the grapevine. The job of management is to encourage upward communication, so that employees feel free to speak to their superiors, and to monitor downward communication continually so that all messages are relevant, accurate, and timely. The most serious problem in downward communication is lag time in the distribution of information. Ideally, every assigned receiver of a common message should receive it at approximately the same time.

Allen (1977) suggests that there are four keys to aligning the formal and informal channels of communication so as to make the most of a network and create a polished, refined process of business communication:

1. A genuine two-way communication flow should be supported at all levels of an organization. As we noted earlier, the formal structure works against a free flow of messages because of its size and arrangement. Therefore, critical issues and messages must flow first, and employees must know that a two-way flow of all messages is sanctioned, encouraged, and possible.

2. The key to sanctioning upward communication is a superior's accessibility and responsiveness as a listener. When supervisors, managers, or employees have problems or requests, they need to know that the boss will listen and act.

3. New or different ideas for changing and improving job conditions or procedures require upward tolerance. Whether the idea is accepted or rejected, a visible, verbal reward for sheer interest is an important message that management can provide.

4. In an atmosphere of positive regard for criticism, suggestions, and the like, management and labor can share in somewhat equal proportions the responsibility for making the system work.

Communication is the central activity of all organizational and business behavior. The people who build their jobs or careers within the formal system are bound together to achieve common goals. Management—the middle and top levels of the network—is charged with the duty of coordinating and focusing an organization's activities and communication (internal and external) on the accomplishment of those goals. The effectiveness of an organization thus depends on the effectiveness of its internal communication activities.

In Chapter 3, we will discuss the kinds of communication skills required in business and industry. Here, it will suffice to say that a wide range of skills is required at all levels to make the system function and produce a profit, in both human and monetary terms.

SUMMARY

In this chapter we stressed the importance of knowing why formal networks have developed in modern business and why businesses preserve certain norms to maintain their existence. We then outlined and briefly discussed seven basic facts about business communication based on the formal network. Next, we defined the communication process in business as personal and transactional. The classification of downward and upward written and oral communication into task and human messages was developed in some detail. Finally, we suggested four keys to aligning the formal and informal channels of communication so as to make the most of a network and of the process of business communication.

EXERCISES

1. Discuss or prepare a paper describing your experience in a grapevine situation. Where were you in the chain illustrated in Figure 1.2? How accurate was the grapevine information when all the facts were known? How did the most affected people in the grapevine react during the chaining out of the message? Most important, what was the nature of people's communication style in the grapevine, and did it vary from their everyday communication styles?

2. Receiving any kind of downward communication or feedback is preferable to receiving none at all. Discuss or prepare a paper about an employment period in which you received little communication. How did you feel when you were given a task and then left alone, with little or no supervision?

3. Constant downward communication eventually can be damaging to one's mental and physical health. Discuss or prepare a paper describing an employment period in which you were hounded by a supervisor or manager. As in exercise 2, describe your feelings about how you were treated.

4. Discuss or prepare a paper on the employment period in which you worked for a *good* manager. Using the information dis-

cussed in Chapter 1, outline and discuss his or her communication skills.

5. Based on your reading of Chapter 1, especially the section on downward communication, write a brief critique of the communication exchange in the following case study. Briefly elaborate on how you might have altered the communication if you were Mr. Daysworth.

Case study: The Jester Company

It is a Friday afternoon in the office of John Daysworth, production supervisor for The Jester Company.

SUSAN: You called for me, Mr. Daysworth?

DAYSWORTH: Yes, Susan. I realize you are still new on our staff, but you are just not producing the amount of work that you should. As you know, we have a one-month probationary employment period before a person is hired permanently. You are in your third week and I must tell you that you simply are going to have to bring your production level up or I won't be able to recommend you for permanent employment.

SUSAN: I'm really trying very hard, Mr. Daysworth.

DAYSWORTH: I'm sure you are. Nevertheless, you simply must put out more production if we are to hire you permanently.

SUSAN: Well, one of my problems is that I am constantly shifted from job to job. I just get going on one thing and I get switched to another.

DAYSWORTH: Yes, I imagine that is a problem.

SUSAN: And I feel like everyone is standing over me all the time. The pressure on me is really more than I can take.

DAYSWORTH: Well, this is all company procedure. We try to scrutinize and evaluate our new employees during the probationary period—and we try to give them exposure to a number of different jobs. Hang in there and do the best you can.

SUSAN: Like I said, I really am trying, Mr. Daysworth.

DAYSWORTH: Think about it over the weekend and try to give it all you've got next week. Remember, the bottom line is production—and your production really must increase.

SUSAN: Okay, Mr. Daysworth.

The following Monday morning, Mr. Daysworth realizes that Susan is not at work. A short time later he receives a phone call from the personnel office informing him that Susan had called to say that she was quitting her job. She gave no reason for quitting.

REFERENCES AND SUGGESTED READINGS

Allen, Richard. 1977. *Organizational Management Through Communication.* New York: Harper & Row. Pp. 53, 58–59.

Baird, John, Jr. 1977. *The Dynamics of Organizational Communication.* New York: Harper & Row. Pp. 1–3.

Caplow, Theodore. 1964. *Principles of Organizations.* New York: Harcourt Brace Jovanovich. Pp. 26–27.

Harris, Linda, and Cronen, Vernon E. 1979. "A Rules-Based Model for the Analysis and Evaluation of Organizational Communications." *Communication Quarterly* 27 (Winter): 20–21.

Katz, Daniel, and Kahn, Robert L. 1966. *The Social Psychology of Organizations.* New York: Wiley. P. 239.

Thayer, Lee. 1968. *Communication and Communication Systems.* Homewood, Ill.: Winard.

Chapter 2

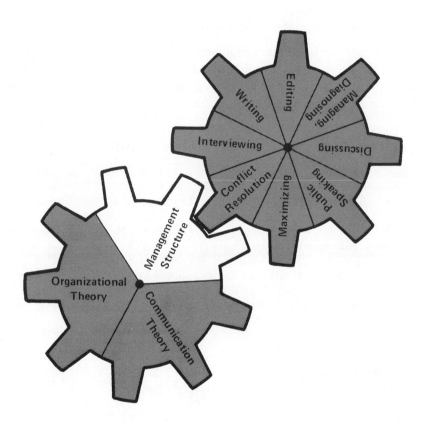

COMMUNICATION
RESPONSIBILITIES
IN BUSINESS

This chapter will provide you with the following:

1. an understanding of the challenging communication demands of middle- and lower-range management

2. an understanding that the communication nerve center of an organization is the interpersonal link between manager and employee

3. the ability to list and discuss the five major communication crises facing business

4. the ability to list and discuss the five general research findings of what managers and employees want on the job

Throughout this book, we stress that organizational or business communication is the sharing of messages, ideas, or attitudes that occur at the work place. For a number of years, the business community has viewed communication as a tool for improving profit and reducing loss. In the past few years, however, communication has come to be viewed also as an aid to increasing productivity among employees.

The most crucial arena of employee communication is now found in middle- and lower-range management. Recent college graduates are increasingly being offered managerial training opportunities—so-called management training programs—in which the challenge of management and the accompanying risks are clearly stated. We shall examine here the assets, the liabilities, and the subsequent responsibilities of management.

MANAGEMENT: RISK, RESPONSIBILITY, AND REWARD

Middle- and lower-range managers have perhaps the most challenging problem in the formal organizational structure. They must look two ways in the organization. First, they must discover and understand what those above them require of them, and secondly, they must act to motivate and persuade those below them to work toward achieving the goals of the organization. Often, someone is disappointed—usually the subordinate rather than the boss.

The crucial task of lower and middle management is to decode organizational goals into everyday work loads so that the organization can function at a high level of productivity. Once the goals are clear and the timetables are set, the manager must decide on a set of communication strategies that take into account the people involved, their job skill levels, and their abilities to perform.

Thus, the tasks of management are bound up in the flow of communication. The obvious first step is knowing how to train en-

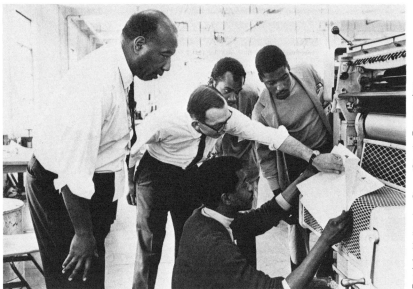

The communication link between supervisor and employee—nerve center of modern business

try-level employees and on-the-job personnel to have skills in communication and management. This book is designed to explain to you the business communication skills expected by business so that you will be able to understand and learn them.

The responsibilities of effective business communication, though few in number, are major in importance. Communication is central to controlling information in business, setting objectives, training personnel, and evaluating performance. The sum total of an organization's daily activities consists of teaching, planning, and rewarding good work. Perhaps nowhere else in the formal channels of modern business are the normal, daily demands of work so clear as they are in the relationship of a manager to his or her employees.

The location of the *action* in a business—the communication nerve center—is the interpersonal connection between the manager or supervisor and the employee. The *reward* of the relationships up and down the channels is a successful business. Many situations and problems can get in the way of an effective series of relationships in business, however. Problems are to be expected, and you must be prepared to meet them.

BARRIERS TO RESPONSIBLE BUSINESS COMMUNICATION

This chapter deals generally with the major communication crises facing business, its managers, and their employees. Chapter 8 will provide a more detailed treatment of the specific areas of conflict and the strategies for dealing with these problems.

Information overload

Even mentioning the issue of information overload adds to the problem. We are all swamped with oral and written material, most of it ill timed to have the desired impact. Although we invite some of the problem, we are often bowled over by the uninvited load of paper. Without a mixed channel approach, one important communication (among many messages) sent in one channel is often lost in our memory and in our priorities.

Information redundancy

A single message is often sent in a variety of ways—through formal channels, in a newsletter, on a bulletin board, and so on. A good idea for using a combination of letters, phone calls, and other channels to get a message across might lead to an unexpected overkill and thus not achieve its goal. As a result, future important employee communications might fall on deaf ears.

Too many links in the formal structure

Although it may seem obvious, we must mention that a large, multileveled organization structure is likely to have more difficulty in employee communication. The greater the distance between up-

21

BARRIERS TO RESPONSIBLE BUSINESS COMMUNICATION

ward and downward communication, the greater the number of communication problems will be. The only solid relationships available to unite the various links may well be those of the manager and subordinate and their peer groups.

Message ownership

A major problem in organizations is that of one specialist delivering to another specialist a message that *belongs* to the first specialist. Just as a vice-president of internal communications cannot be responsible for everyone's communication problems, no one person can *own* a problem or keep the message away from others. Assuming too much responsibility for someone else's communication success or refusing to share a portion of the load because the problem *belongs* to someone else is an example of this barrier to responsible business communication.

Message ambiguity

If message senders and receivers are ignorant of the most simple concepts and skills of communication, the business environment is in serious trouble. Inability to interpret nonverbal behavior, imprecision with language, omission of important items in a training program, and, most crucial, *uncertainty* on the part of the sender can lead to lost time, lost profit, and lost relationships.

Overcoming the barriers

In all these matters, it is clear that the real losers are the company leaders who entrust their managers and supervisors with making the company *work*. Systematic and careful attention to developing good communication between management and labor can reduce the normal flow of conflict in the business environment to an acceptable level.

A business will continue to produce what it was created to produce—a restaurant will produce food, a power company will supply power to its customers, and so on. With the increasing prices of food and fuel, employee demands for higher wages, and consumer outcry against higher rates, however, will come a steady evolution and change *within* the business.

The most important question evolving from attention to the barriers to responsible business communication and to the nature of change in the business system is how business, management, and labor can serve as agents of change. It is clear that businesses cannot wait for change and merely react to it, nor can they engage in crisis techniques of communication every time a problem flares up somewhere in the formal business system.

To attain a reasonably steady state of responsible change in a business, there must be an awareness of the communication needs of management and labor: what people want from their jobs and what the determinants of job satisfaction are for management and labor. These and other communication questions are important considerations for you as you look ahead to the marketplace and the real world of business.

WHAT MANAGERS AND EMPLOYEES WANT ON THE JOB

The responsibility of management is to design and implement specific communication activities, send information, establish good relationships, and provide a work place that is safe and comfortable. This is not to say that everything is beautiful in employer-employee relationships; in some situations, it is far from the truth.

Goldhaber and associates (1978) researched the broad questions of communication effectiveness (upward and downward) in business and organization.[1] Their findings are especially useful in our consideration of responsible communication.

The Goldhaber study found that employees want more infor-

---

[1] Goldhaber's work spanned sixteen organizations and involved 3,931 respondents, of whom 60 percent were salaried female nonsupervisors under forty years of age. All of the respondents indicated that they talked with more than five people in a work day. The sample showed a higher turnover rate (a modern fact of life); 56 percent had worked for their present organization for fewer than five years and 72 percent had been in their present jobs for fewer than five years.

mation about organizational concerns (decisions that affect their jobs, mistakes and failures, and problems of management). Employees surveyed claimed that they already received adequate information about job requirements, pay, and benefits but that they wanted more information about company matters that would affect them.

Employees want the opportunity to send information to others. The survey revealed that rather than complaints or gripes, employees want more information on how to do their jobs, and they want reports on job progress.

The surveyed employees also wanted more information from sources closest to them—peers, supervisor, or manager. Because employees believe they received less information from distant sources—and they may not want to hear from the top levels—they rely on the grapevine.

It is important that quality information be received on time. Information from distant sources was generally considered to be of lower quality than that from closer sources. The most accurate and timely information tended to come from co-workers and supervisors rather than from top management. The survey revealed that top management, from whom only one-third of the respondents claimed they received timely information, was the real culprit. The continued use of the grapevine, a fast channel with a low-quality message, was the employees' answer to a wish for more information, primarily because information from top management arrived either too early or too late.

Employees also want more face-to-face contacts. Over half of the survey respondents indicated that they received most of their information from face-to-face contacts and written channels, rather than by telephone. Nearly two-thirds of the respondents wanted more interpersonal contact, especially in meetings with top management and immediate supervisors.

In general, the Goldhaber survey discovered that, among all the companies and the respondents, the *immediate* communication climate—co-workers, supervisors, and managers—was excellent. Most of the respondents liked where they worked and liked the people around them. The immediate work place seemed to fos-

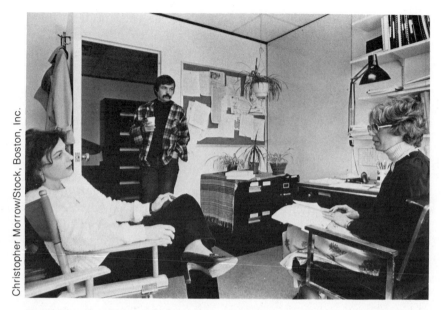

Christopher Morrow/Stock, Boston, Inc.

Communication is a personal business transaction—a shared process of feelings and ideas

ter solid interpersonal relations, whereas the organization as a whole was not nearly so reliable in the flow of information and in its trust for and in the employee.

Employees in the Goldhaber survey seemed to feel that they had gone as far as possible in their organization, perhaps because they had not received sufficient information about how they fitted into the organization. It must be noted, however, that the survey itself or insufficient reward systems, performance appraisal interviews, and other feedback devices may have contributed to the dissatisfaction of the survey respondents.

We can conclude, then, that employees want several basic items from their employers:

1. the necessities of life—a fair wage
2. fair treatment
3. knowledge of what is expected of them

4. individual recognition
5. a chance to succeed

You will find that the major communication responsibility of a business rests with the immediate supervisor or manager and the employees. If their relationship is solid, if it is marked by trust and understanding, then the business or organization is fulfilling most of its tangible and intangible obligations to its workers. Rarely is a business or organization so secure that it can do without trust and understanding between labor and management.

The formally structured communication system of an organization can develop by meeting schedules and by establishing follow-up procedures, accurate and timely messages, and the methods necessary for dispensing and receiving information from within quickly. Finally, a business must also be responsible for showing its workers more about how the business functions and how each person may move up the ladder of success and for making it clear to them that the business knows where it is going.

SUMMARY

In this chapter we focused on the risks and rewards of management as they are bound up in the flow of communication. We then discussed five areas of communication conflict between managers and their employees. Since managers are also employees, we presented the findings of a study concerning what employees want from their jobs. We concluded by discussing the major communication responsibility of a business and how the business or organization must set timely and accurate procedures for dispensing information about its functions.

EXERCISES

1. Discuss or prepare a paper describing your personal experience or an observed experience of a visible reward for an employee. As you share your experience, pay particular attention to the communication climate in which the reward occurred.
2. Using the barriers to responsible business communication

covered in this chapter as your guide, discuss or prepare a paper describing troublesome experiences you have had in a part-time or full-time employment situation.

3. Based on your experience, discuss or prepare a paper on what employees *really* want most in their work place. Are your findings similar in rank and subject matter to those of the Goldhaber study?

4. Based on your reading of Chapter 2, especially the section on message ambiguity and face-to-face communication, write a brief critique of the following case study. Briefly describe alternative ways you might have handled this communication if you were Mr. Smith.

Case study: Belford Manufacturing Company

SMITH: I can't believe that. You've got to be kidding.

RADAR: Why would I be kidding you? Hey, for Pete's sake, it's the honest truth. She sent me a resume and asked if we still had any job openings. She said she would like to reconsider our company.

SMITH: Judy is one of our finest new employees. I really highly treasure her in our organization. We gave her a salary adjustment at the end of her three-month probationary period and she seemed very pleased. I am in contact with her every few days and she always seems very happy in her job. I just can't believe that Judy would have done that.

RADAR: Sorry, friend, but that's the way it is. For a price, I can make sure her application doesn't go any further. Just kidding, of course. Really, Smitty, you don't need to worry about it. We don't have anything available for her right now and, anyway, we wouldn't look with favor on an application like this so soon after she rejected our offer. You lucky guys won out when we both offered her jobs, so now she's yours.

SMITH: Thanks, pal, but I still wonder why Judy would have done that.

RADAR: Well, I'll leave that to you. Just thought I'd pass the info along to you. These personnel association meetings ought to be worth something!

Smith returned to the plant from his meeting and immediately called for Judy.

JUDY: You called for me, Mr. Smith?

SMITH: Yes, come right in. Judy, I have just learned that you might be job hunting. I'm quite upset. I consider you one of our very finest new employees and have told you this on several occasions. I even got you a big salary increase at the end of your probationary period. What's up?

JUDY: You've got to keep your options open, Mr. Smith. I have to work to support my family. I can't afford to be laid off or be without a job. In your memo last week you mentioned that orders were down and that we would have to cut costs drastically. When you said we should prepare for the worst, well . . . I decided it was time to start looking.

SMITH: Well, I certainly didn't have you in mind, Judy. Some others maybe, but not you. It depends on what happens in sales, but all of us, including myself, have got to hold down costs.

JUDY: As one of the newer employees, I realize that company policy dictates that I go early. "Last in, first out," you know.

SMITH: That's a general company policy.

JUDY: I certainly appreciate your encouraging words today, Mr. Smith. Like I said, I really must work. I feel better after talking with you about this.

REFERENCES AND SUGGESTED READINGS

Allen, Richard. 1977. *Organizational Management Through Communication.* New York: Harper & Row. P. 40 ff.

Goldhaber, Gerald, ed. 1978. *Organizational Outcomes as a Function of Communication Effectiveness.* San Francisco: Academy of Management, August.

Lewis, Phillip V. 1977. *Organizational Communication: The Essence of Effective Management.* Columbus, Ohio: Grid. P. 45 ff.

Chapter 3

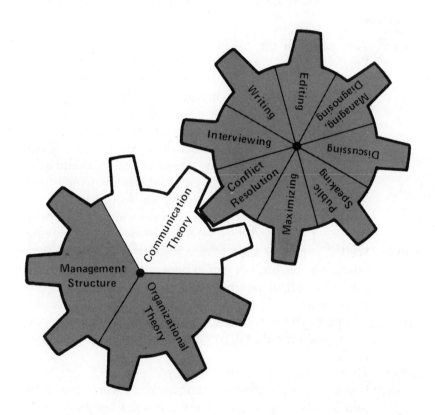

COMMUNICATION COMPETENCES IN BUSINESS

This chapter will provide you with the following:

1. an understanding of the vital importance of communication *skills* to American business

2. the ability to outline and discuss the career graph indicating the nature, types, and forms of communication from job entry to retirement

3. the ability to distinguish between a *skill* and a *competence*

4. the ability to list the frequency of use of communication skills at the entry job level

5. the ability to distinguish the range and priority of skills necessary for communicating upward and downward

6. the ability to list and discuss the central elements of communication competence in business

7. the ability to list and discuss the five skills necessary for interpersonal competence

8. the ability to distinguish minimal, satisfactory, and optimal communication competence

As we move toward the twenty-first century, the importance of specific communication skills in American business may well become the number one priority of our working lives. Numerous researchers already have found that from 50 to 60 percent of *every* worker's time is consumed in oral or written communication (Baird, 1977). Depending on the type of business, the nature of the specific job, and so on, the real time on the job spent in sending or receiving messages may be even higher than 60 percent. The point is simple but with profound impact. If you wish to have a meaningful and progressive career in your chosen field, you must learn and bring to your entry job level performance a comprehensive set of oral and written communication skills. Moreover, you must learn to be adaptive in your subsequent acquisition of *in-depth* specific communication skills as they are required on the job.

COMMUNICATION SKILLS: EFFECTIVENESS AT THE ENTRY JOB LEVEL

The speech communication profession, through courses and programs in business or organizational communication, provides instruction primarily for those at the entry job level. Table 3.1 outlines a speculative, but reasonably accurate, picture of the communication dimensions of a career from college graduation to retirement. Those in the speech communication profession know very little about the communication demands and problems of phases II and III, except what we have learned and what we are currently learning as teachers or consultants. What we do learn about these mature years in career life cycles in business and industry is usually applied to advanced programs of study in organizational communication. In this text, with our interests in your preparation for the real world of business, we will focus our efforts on phase I.

In the past, college and university graduates usually have not received proper preparation in communication skills for adequate entry job level performance. In recent years, however, this un-

Table 3.1 Speech communication as applied to jobs and careers

PHASE I	PHASE II	PHASE III
1–8 years after graduation	9–12 years	13 years to retirement
General and particularized applications of spoken and written skills are necessary to fulfill entry job level requirements. Gradually, one or more skills will dominate the work place experience. Speech programs prepare the student for only the early years of phase I.	The profession knows little about the communication demands and constraints of phase II because curricula do not address this unknown area. Toward the end of phase II, staffs seek retraining in traditional speech skills (public and group). At the managerial and supervisory levels, in-house and consultant services are most active, dealing mainly with specific company needs (arbitration, problem solving, staff harmony, and teaching old skills to inadequately pretrained personnel).	Phase III consists of retraining in standard and specialized skills as the employee gains established levels of job responsibility. Involvement in continuing education unit (CEU) courses in public speaking and in allied communication areas is common. The profession knows little about phase III communication demands.

happy circumstance has changed systematically. Now and in the future, we believe that you can be assured of a responsive communication education in your college career. We are dedicated to that challenge.

First, we will discuss some general and specific answers to the following important questions:

1. What are the communication skills at the entry job level in which you need preparation?
2. What are the communication competences at the entry job level for which you need preparation?

The differences between *skills* and *competences* are subtle. We will differentiate between these two terms by defining *skills* as performance-based expressions of spoken or written communication—that is, information giving and receiving, listening abilities, self-expression, and so on. *Competences* in communication are the levels of *mastery* or *control* that you have in a communication situation, ranging from minimal, to satisfactory, to optimal. Control is not something that you do *to* others; rather, it is something you do *for* and *with* others. We will discuss these distinctions later in more detail. For now, we will deal first with the skills required and then with the levels of competence desired by business and industry.

Several studies have highlighted the communication skills required at the entry job level. Table 3.2 shows the results of an Ohio University study into the skills used by first-year employees (Huegli and Tschirgi, 1974). Note that most of these skills focus on interpersonal conferences with superiors and with peers. Huegli and Tschirgi argue that entry level positions seldom afford interaction with customers, suppliers, or the public at large. Their survey further reveals that almost all supervisors interviewed noted that entry level employees were deficient in *communication skills application*. As we suggested in Table 3.1, phases II and III require greater expertise in more complex and more challenging communication problems. In phase I—and in the data shown in Table 3.2—the frequency of different kinds of communication skills at

Table 3.2 Communication skills: Frequency of use and importance at the entry job level for first-year employees

| | FREQUENCY | | IMPORTANCE |
SKILL	VERY OFTEN	OCCASIONALLY	RANKING
Conferences with boss about my work	43	34	82
Conferences with others at same level	46	31	28
Listening to boss's ideas and suggestions	32	36	68
Selling my ideas to others face to face	39	31	70
Conferences with subordinates about their work	22	26	48
Written reports to boss about my work	16	27	43
Written proposals for new action for my organization	13	29	42
Selling my ideas in written reports	8	23	41
Written requests for information to others in organization	15	26	41
Written technical reports	20	20	40
Conferences with customers about selling products or services	18	16	34
Conferences with suppliers	10	18	28
Making public appearances and giving speeches	1	8	9

Source: Jon M. Huegli and Harvey D. Tschirgi, "An Investigation of Communication Skills Application and Effectiveness at the Entry Job Level," *The Journal of Business Communication* 12 (Fall 1974): 25. Reprinted by permission.

the entry job level suggests more implementation of oral or speech communication skills than of written communication skills.

In a related and even broader survey conducted at the University of Nebraska at Lincoln, DiSalvo, Larsen, and Seiler (1976) addressed the same question: what communication skills are needed by persons in business organizations at all levels. Table 3.3 indicates that the respondents rated listening (average rating, 3.79), routine information exchange (3.46), and advising (3.23) as the most important communication activities, regardless of whether

Table 3.3 Importance of type of communication skill by organizational direction

TYPE OF COMMUNICATION	DIRECTION OF COMMUNICATION				
	UP	DOWN	WITHIN	OUTSIDE	AVERAGE
Advising	3.05	3.35	3.38	3.14	3.23
Persuading	2.95	2.84	3.05	3.14	2.99
Instructing	1.60	3.38	3.06	2.67	2.67
Interviewing	1.07	2.02	1.66	2.25	1.75
Routine information exchange	3.41	3.38	3.74	3.34	3.46
Public speaking	1.44	1.51	1.58	2.19	1.68
Small group/conference leadership	2.14	2.42	2.69	2.40	2.41
Giving orders	0.78	3.19	2.51	1.55	2.00
Small group/conference problem solving	2.72	2.81	3.16	2.52	2.80
Listening	3.90	3.46	3.82	4.00	3.79

$N = 170$. Ratings are mean ratings based on a scale of 1–5, with 1 as the lowest rating and 5 as the highest.
Source: See Vincent DiSalvo, David C. Larson, and William J. Seiler, "Communication Skills Needed by Persons in Business Organizations," *Communication Education* 25 (November 1976): 269–275.

the communication was to someone up the channel, down the channel, within the rank, or outside the work group.

DiSalvo, Larsen, and Seiler focused their attention on two job classifications among the graduates involved in the survey—finance-oriented jobs and personnel-oriented jobs. Ratings by those in finance-oriented positions (Table 3.4) show that listening (3.69) and routine information exchange (3.27) are the most important types, regardless of the channel direction. In addition, people in finance positions instruct (3.04) more with people below them, problem solve (3.02) and advise (3.02) more with people within their work group, and persuade (3.14) more with people outside their work group.

Those in personnel-oriented positions (Table 3.5) indicate that listening (3.97), advising (3.78), routine information exchange (3.60), and persuading (3.42) are important skills with employees above them. When the direction of communication shifted to employees below them, they rated instructing (4.04), listening (3.78), advising (3.76), giving orders (3.66), and small group prob-

Table 3.4 Importance of type of communication skill by organizational direction for finance-oriented positions

	DIRECTION OF COMMUNICATION				
TYPE OF COMMUNICATION	UP	DOWN	WITHIN	OUTSIDE	AVERAGE
Advising	2.74	2.94	3.02	2.94	2.91
Persuading	2.80	2.36	2.68	3.14	2.75
Instructing	1.64	3.04	2.76	2.68	2.53
Interviewing	0.94	2.18	1.08	1.82	1.51
Routine information exchange	3.36	3.10	3.38	3.22	3.27
Public speaking	1.00	1.12	1.00	1.80	1.23
Small group/conference leadership	2.00	2.22	2.32	2.34	2.22
Giving orders	0.80	2.70	2.20	1.86	1.89
Small group/conference problem solving	2.84	2.74	3.02	2.58	2.80
Listening	3.88	3.26	3.70	3.92	3.69

$N = 50$. Ratings are mean ratings based on a scale of 1–5, with 1 as the lowest rating and 5 as the highest.
Source: See Vincent DiSalvo, David C. Larson, and William J. Seiler, "Communication Skills Needed by Persons in Business Organizations," *Communication Education* 25 (November 1976): 269–275.

Table 3.5 Importance of type of communication skill by organizational direction for personnel-oriented positions

	DIRECTION OF COMMUNICATION				
TYPE OF COMMUNICATION	UP	DOWN	WITHIN	OUTSIDE	AVERAGE
Advising	3.78	3.76	3.87	2.91	3.58
Persuading	3.42	3.34	3.48	2.93	3.29
Instructing	1.62	4.04	3.40	2.26	2.83
Interviewing	1.23	2.72	2.21	2.36	2.13
Routine information exchange	3.60	3.55	3.91	3.19	3.56
Public speaking	1.93	1.72	1.91	2.26	1.96
Small group/conference leadership	2.40	2.76	3.04	3.38	2.90
Giving orders	0.78	3.66	2.87	1.40	2.18
Small group/conference problem solving	2.96	3.06	3.20	2.55	2.94
Listening	3.97	3.78	3.87	4.00	3.91

$N = 47$. Ratings are mean ratings based on a scale of 1–5, with 1 as the lowest rating and 5 as the highest.
Source: See Vincent DiSalvo, David C. Larson, and William J. Seiler, "Communication Skills Needed by Persons in Business Organizations," *Communication Education* 25 (November 1976): 269–275.

lem solving (3.06) as most important. For communication with people within the work group, routine information exchange (3.91) and small group leadership (3.04) were noted as important. For communication outside the work group, listening (4.00), small group leadership (3.38), and routine information exchange (3.19) were important.

The results of another DiSalvo, Larsen, and Seiler (1976) survey are extremely important to you at this early point in your course of study. When the respondents were asked what they *wished* they had been taught in college, they answered as follows:

1. listening
2. public speaking and presentation of technical information
3. writing
4. small group leadership and problem-solving communication
5. human relations
6. persuasion and attitude theory

The message is clear. Spoken and written communication skills at the entry job level are specifically required and widely used, and they vary in nature and in type from channel to channel and from job level to job level.

In summary, you will need to fulfill the following four criteria to translate into practice what you will learn about communication theory and practice:

1. You must be knowledgeable in a broad range of communication processes and skills.
2. You must be well grounded in theories—why a communication situation is as it is and why it is as complex as it is.
3. You must be able to bridge the gap between theory and application.
4. You must be knowledgeable about the business environment.

COMMUNICATION COMPETENCE

As we mentioned earlier, the general character of competence in communication is difficult to distinguish. We can define its central elements, however, with some degree of certainty.

Michael D. Sullivan

Communication skills occupy the most important parts of our day

First, you must be able to specify and control your communication environment so as to realize certain rewards or goals. The competent communicator is one who maximizes goal attainment. The implication here is that other parties in the communication environment will not necessarily be involved in measuring your competence or be critical of its success. The degrees of sensitivity and control are mutual, but it is mainly up to *you* to achieve your own goals.

Parks (1977) argues that you will be competent when you are (1) aware of your communication goals, (2) able to articulate those goals with a moderate to high level of specificity, and (3) able to account for their potential for success or failure throughout the communication situation.

Communication competence also involves the ability to draw upon a substantial stock of strategies to employ in communication situations and the sensitivity to select the appropriate strategies to meet others' needs for silence, jargon, clarity, ambiguity, and so on. In short, there are times to "tell it like it is" and times to be subtle or silent.

Finally, assessing competence in communication in both private and business settings involves two questions: Did you achieve your goals? Were your goals right or desirable? These questions are not easy to answer in communication settings because of the variety of constraints and inhibitions that can exist between people. A supervisor or manager may want to discipline or punish a subordinate in an appraisal interview, for example, or an employee may want to submit a grievance to a superior.

The assessment of communication competence in business may well rest on an individual's interpersonal communication capabilities and communication maturity. Bochner and Kelly (1974) have isolated five skills that are necessary for interpersonal communication competence:

1. *Empathic communication:* The measure of competence here is in assessing your capacity to identify correctly the emotions communicated to you through verbal and nonverbal channels.

2. *Descriptiveness:* In the process of giving and receiving feedback, the measure of competence is the specific, descriptive, and concrete verbal and nonverbal language you use to relate to others.

3. *Ownership of feelings and thoughts:* Ownership requires that you identify and communicate to others the attitudes and feelings that belong to you.

4. *Self-disclosure:* Communication that shares what you really feel, think, or want is self-disclosure. A measure of competence at this level of communication is whether or not it is right and desirable to reveal your inner self voluntarily.

5. *Behavioral flexibility:* The competent communicator behaves in a way that is appropriate to the communication situation. Your flexibility to vary your output is directly related to your skills, capabilities, and the developing requirements of your life-style and your job.

DEMONSTRATING AND ASSESSING COMPETENCE

The next step in the process of your acquisition of communication skills is to develop methods for assessing *demonstrated competences* in business communication by (1) learning the dimensions of oral and written skills, and (2) learning to measure these skills through performance exercises or simulation and written examinations.

Levison (1976) explains that assessment of competence requires the establishment of behavioral objectives: what you do while demonstrating competence and what the standards of performance and written acceptability are—that is, the minimal level of competence. In Part II of this book, keeping in mind the requirement of performing at a minimal level of communication competence, you will be asked the following:

1. What activities will be undertaken to demonstrate competence?
2. What are the conditions under which the performance takes place?
3. What are the criteria for successfully completing the behavioral objective of demonstrating minimal competence?

In other words, we want you to be able to demonstrate—through your general spoken and written communication performance and through testing—that you "know what you know."

In a business or organizational system, you will find that you move from one level to another in your communication competence—*minimal, satisfactory,* and *optimal.* In any job, this movement is a kind of interpersonal and intellectual measurement of how you are learning and growing with the organization. We agree with Harris and Cronen's (1979) assessment of levels of communication competence, because it fits in well with our concerns in the preceding pages. We interpret Harris and Cronen's levels as follows:

1. *Minimal competence:* Whether briefly or for the duration of employment, the minimally competent communicator knows the simple mechanics and communication rules necessary for day-to-day job performance. This person obeys

the rules but knows little about the organizational structure and does not know or care to learn how to go up the ladder of success.

2. *Satisfactory competence:* The satisfactorily competent communicator has learned the nature and function of the organization of which he or she is a part. The goals of the company become the communicator's goals, although his or her skills are not sufficiently developed for company leadership. On the personal and organizational level, the satisfactorily competent communicator can make adequate short-term decisions and function adequately in a conflict-arousing setting, but he or she cannot see beyond the short term for the long-term benefits of a personal and a business communication situation.

3. *Optimal competence:* Harris and Cronen suggest that a high level of communication competence implies the ability to know the rules of organization, its objectives, and its goals and the ability to assess *options* to those rules, objectives, and goals. The optimal communicator *creates* answers to problems where none had existed before. He or she can detect discord in an office, and, by understanding the rules, procedures, and objectives of the company, can structure a fitting response or answer.

It is obvious that there will be a difference in your levels of competence now and your potential for improvement as you learn and experience the demands of business communication. In a given situation, you may be strategically competent because you know what is wrong but minimally competent in your ability to do something about the problem.

SUMMARY

Competence in communication relationships is an important concept for success in business. In this chapter, we have broadly outlined the elements of spoken, written, and nonverbal communication that are important to American business and industry. The materials and substance of this book are designed to assist your development as a minimally to satisfactorily competent communicator, with the ability to see your everyday communication demands through the eyes of the optimal communicator. As you progress through the three career phases described in Table 3.1, we believe that you will become an optimally competent communicator. We would certainly hope for such a worthy goal. The requirements of the entry job level in Table 3.1 roughly parallel the progression of competence in communication behaviors detailed by Harris and Cronen.

The eight chapters in Part II detail the fundamental communication skills that are necessary to perform business tasks. The exercises in those chapters should help to provide direction and purpose to your awareness and acquisition of the wide range of communication functions that are important to the success of contemporary business.

EXERCISES

Prepare a written report, a group presentation, or an informative speech on any of these exercises.

1. Conduct a survey of local managers (from several types of businesses, such as supermarkets, fast-food chains, light industry) regarding the content of conferences with their employees about work. What do these bosses say to their employees? What do they see as their communication obligations to their employees? Do they believe they should be directive, situational, or autocratic leaders? Generally, you should discover all you can about the communication content and style of the bosses you interview.

2. In a survey similar to that in exercise 1, ask the managers about the communication skills or deficiencies they see in their employees. Compare your findings with the tables in this chapter.

3. To enhance our discussion of minimal, satisfactory, and optimal communication competence, interview one local business organization's chief executive officer about his or her staff. Inquire about the levels of communication abilities among the

staff, using the suggested guidelines in this chapter. Your instructor can assist you in sorting out the subtleties among the three categories of competence. This assignment may be the most difficult of the three exercises related to your understanding of how you and others can learn to control your communication experiences.

4. Write a brief explanation of how effective communication played an important role in helping to increase productivity in the following case study.

Case study: Barker Industries

Edward Johnson, plant manager, has been frustrated by the poor productivity of the finishing division of his plant. Numerous changes have been implemented over the past several years to try to improve productivity. Recently, Johnson promoted Jerry Knowles to supervisor of this troubled division.

After several weeks on the job as supervisor, Knowles developed a plan of action, which he submitted to Ed Johnson. Johnson wasn't sure about the idea, but at this stage he was willing to let just about anything be tried to improve the productivity of this division. Thus, with Johnson's reluctant blessing, Knowles implemented his new plan. Briefly, the new plan consisted of allowing each worker in the division to develop personal job productivity goals. Each worker was to meet with Knowles and discuss his or her job and what he or she considered a realistic productivity goal. Then, each week, each employee would meet with Knowles to go over the results of the past week. Workers who met their production goals would get quality points. Once each month the quality points would be added up, and a cash bonus based on the number of monthly quality points would be awarded. Problems identified in the weekly meetings could be dealt with by Knowles to help the workers achieve their goals.

After gaining approval for the plan from Johnson, Knowles held a meeting with all his production employees to explain the program. Knowles asked for the reactions and suggestions of his employees. His employees suggested that the meetings occur every other week rather than weekly and asked to elect a three-member committee to help deal with identified problems that hampered productivity. Knowles agreed to these changes.

After the program had been in operation for only three months, Johnson noticed a dramatic turnaround in the productivity of Knowles's division. The increase ranged from a low of 3 percent to a high of 14 percent, with a 9 percent average increase. Ed Johnson gave all the credit to Jerry Knowles, but Knowles said that it was a team effort and that the credit was due to each worker in his division.

REFERENCES AND SUGGESTED READINGS

Baird, John E., Jr. 1977. *The Dynamics of Organizational Communication.* New York: Harper & Row. Ch. 1.

Bochner, Arthur P., and Kelly, Clifford W. 1974. "Interpersonal Competence: Rationale, Philosophy, and Implementation of a Conceptual Framework," *Speech Teacher* 73 (November): 279–301.

DiSalvo, Vincent, Larson, David C., and Seiler, William J. 1976. "Communication Skills Needed by Persons in Business Organizations." *Communication Education* 25 (November): 269–275.

Harris, Linda, and Vernon E. Cronen. 1979. "A Rules-Based Model for the Analysis and Evaluation of Organizational Communication." *Communication Quarterly* 27 (Winter): 20–21.

Huegli, Jon M., and Tschirgi, Harvey D. 1974. "An Investigation of Communication Skills Application and Effectiveness at the Entry Job Level." *Journal of Business Communication* 12 (Fall): 24–29.

Levison, Gayle K. 1976. "The Basic Speech Communication Course: Establishing Minimal Oral Competencies and Exemption Procedures." *Communication Education* 25 (September): 222–230.

Parks, Malcolm R. 1977. "Issues in the Explication of Communication Competency." Presented at Western Speech Communication Association Convention, Phoenix, November.

PART II

DEVELOPING COMMUNICATION SKILLS

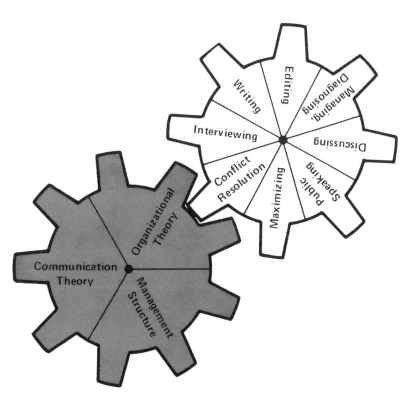

Chapter 4

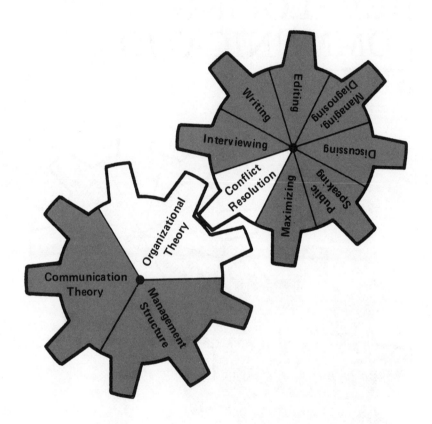

YOU AND YOUR JOB: GETTING ALONG

This chapter will provide you with the following:

1. the ability to define and discuss the quality of life concept in American business

2. the ability to identify five areas of on-the-job conflict

3. the ability to discuss and understand six basic approaches to resolving personal clashes between labor and management or difficulties in getting along on the job

To get along with your fellow employees on the job, you will need to understand the usual day-by-day personality of the modern business organization. The various personalities in the organization often share in the creation of on-the-job conflicts that make for an unpleasant work place and even lead to a downturn in productivity. At other times, the employer and the employee generate their own problems, separate from those of each other. The net result is the same. Problems exist in organizations as an inherent and unfortunately necessary dimension of their formal and informal structures. There are never any easy answers, but there are some starting points whereby conflicts can be understood and managed. This chapter will deal with the major problem areas of phase I, the entry job level (see Chapter 3, Figure 3.1), primarily in the interpersonal domain.

Without question, the quality of work life in today's business world is the most serious problem for both senior and new employees. Although it is defined in various ways, quality of work life means that every job of substance should be challenging, devoted to helping others, and grounded in interpersonal relationships that satisfy the need to be a vital part of the business. These days, the quality of an employee's work place is consistently considered more important than even good pay. These concerns about quality of work life are a far cry from the concerns of the 1950s and 1960s, when good pay and good benefits were the primary appeals to high school and college graduates.

There is so much more to involvement in the work place than money and sick leave policies, although these concerns should not be downplayed. Getting along in phase I involves five conflict areas—a basic set of communication demands placed upon you by your employer and your fellow employees. We shall examine each of these conflict areas in turn.

CONFLICT AREA 1: THE COMMUNICATION SKILLS REQUIRED IN PHASE I

Surveys of employees' interests in communication skills reveal little new information, but the message is clear: they want to develop

1. effective listening skills (a subject that will be developed in Chapter 10)
2. proper pronunciation of standard English, correct grammar, and a clear voice
3. organizational skills for assembling information and orderly thinking and speaking techniques for delivering messages appropriately

These expectations are flexible enough that most entry job level employees should be able to comply. Development of basic communication skills is not an end unto itself, desirable only because it is a good thing for employees to do or because every competing business is doing it. Employees should be effective communicators because the success of any business depends on how well the organization's objectives are understood and how well the understanding of these needs is communicated to the marketplace.

The conflict between employee and employer expectations of entry job level communication skills is that too few entry level workers are skilled in spoken or written communication. The underlying premise of this book is that students preparing for careers in business have been busy learning the intricacies of their chosen fields—accounting, computer science, and so on. The most important dimension of their education—communication training—has evolved into a crash course or two at the last minute. Every chapter of this book has been prepared, therefore, as a warning and as a positive message to counter these prevailing approaches to business education. The entry job level employee must bring to a job a full complement of communication skills as well as course preparation and experience in a specific business skill.

On the job, you will be able to get along better with your supervisor and your organization if you understand some basic facts of business communication. Within every organization four kinds of information must be communicated to every audience in the formal structure of the work place:

1. You need to know the rules, policies, procedures, and practices of your organization. You need to learn them early on and be able to share them with those at your level of the network and those at the level immediately below you.
2. You need to know your business's current progress. Is it producing at maximum levels? If not, why not? Is the current status of the business likely to increase your work load or reduce it? What about the work load of those around you?
3. You need to know the financial history of your business. Is there a pattern of progress or regress in the profit-loss statement? You should learn as much as you can about these matters because they affect the way you feel, speak, and work from day to day.
4. Finally, you need to know where the business is going. What are the organization's plans and objectives, and how do you fit into those plans? The way you are treated about these matters and the way you communicate with your peers are what make for a healthy, open communication atmosphere.

If these four kinds of information are not clearly communicated and understood, then you may be constantly dealing with conflict crises rather than using effective communication to meet the primary needs of getting along on the job.

CONFLICT AREA 2: JOB SATISFACTION OR DISSATISFACTION

People want to be treated as individuals. Unfortunately, many modern organizations do not consider that fact important enough to want to do much about it. A simple premise of good business communication is that, if people were put ahead of product, profit would take care of itself.

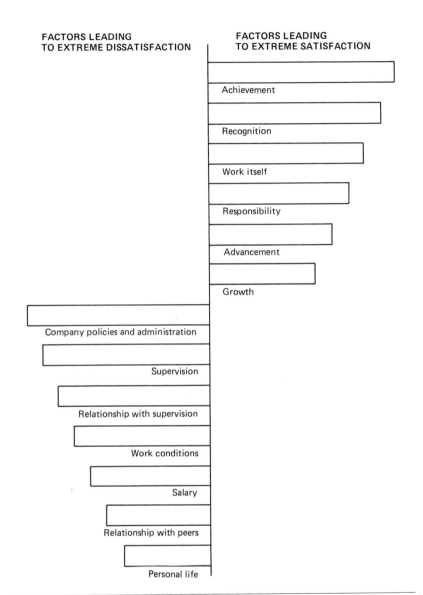

FIGURE 4.1   Factors affecting job attitudes

Source: Reprinted by permission of the *Harvard Business Review.* Exhibit from "One More Time: How Do You Motivate Employees?" by Frederick Herzberg (January/ February 1968). Copyright © 1968 by the President and Fellows of Harvard College; all rights reserved.

As we approach the last decades of the twentieth century, many businesses are beginning to see the light and show some concern for people—the key element that sets one business apart from another. By putting people first, an organization can stay near the top of the competitive heap. The key to job satisfaction is putting the employees first and, with effective supervision, giving them the latitude to do their jobs.

The darker side of employer-employee relations is job dissatisfaction and the swirling winds of conflict in the work place. Herzberg (1968) suggests a set of factors that contribute to job satisfaction and dissatisfaction. Figure 4.1 outlines these areas of concern.

Conflicts that arise between labor and management are perhaps the largest problem area. Labor and management are really on the same side, however; they need each other. Your supervisor or manager and even those in top management are like you in many ways. Everyone who works for someone else wants to be respected, to be understood, to have the freedom to grow and advance, and to be fulfilled in his or her work. When there is a threat to one, therefore, there is a threat to all.

Conflicts among members of an organization are usually communication problems that damage the effective and efficient channels of business operations. Communication problems that lead to conflict occur on four levels:

1. A blockage of the formal communication arteries leads to low levels of routine information exchange and even repression of information. When you learn more about your company's plans from a union report or from the grapevine, you can be sure that serious communication problems are at hand.

2. When the two-way flow of information is severely restricted, you can expect that threats from those around you and from the ranks below you will surface and cause anxiety. These communication battle cries are signs of concern for everyone involved.

3. When you and your colleagues are not involved or asked to express your opinions, you can be sure that communication conflicts will surface. The channel of upward communication may be

nearly closed, but the closure can be opened by all manner of union and government policies. As one company president noted, "They're going to find out one way or another, so we might as well tell it to them straight." Fortunately, such attitudes are becoming less common. Perhaps the issue has been overstated, but you still live in a world where "the boss" thinks he ought to know more than you do and where what you do know comes from carefully selected and filtered messages.

4. The last level involves threats of a more serious nature that lead to fights, to withholding of information, and to nonverbal confrontations with employees who are sending terse communications through the formal, informal, and grapevine networks. It is hoped that these times will be few and far between for you, but strikes, walkouts, sitdowns, shutdowns, and absenteeism are ever-present attacks on the heart of a business.

Management may be doing all it can to maintain a progressive stance on wages, employee recognition, methods of advancement, and so on. If these four levels of communication conflict persist, however, even the best plans can produce few satisfactory solutions. Moreover, some organizations seem to have a contradictory attitude toward management and communication, placing product ahead of people. If you are to experience and ultimately be a part of a better management style, by which creativity and capabilities are fully developed, then you need to be aware of and armed with the communication skills to meet the challenge. Ask yourself this of your job: Am I challenged? Can I grow? Can I advance? Can I achieve? Most important, what can I say or do to help my boss look good?

One important communication philosophy undergirds all that has been said so far and all that remains to be said in this book. It is expressed well on a plaque in the lobby of the Superior Body Works in Lima, Ohio:

> Let your light so shine and a little ahead of the next,
> They have copied all they could copy, but
> They could not copy our minds,
> So, we left them copying and stealing a mile and a half behind.

CONFLICT AREA 3: UNDERESTIMATING GROUP COMMUNICATION SKILLS

Many entry job level employees who are skilled in oral communication inadvertently use those skills as substitutes for written skills, and the trade-off does not work. Most college graduates seeking career entry positions believe that they are better qualified in communication skills than they really are. An integration of all forms of communication skills is not a frill on your resume but is an essential part of your education. Along with a minimun base of skills must come a sensitivity to the interaction of reading, speaking, listening, and nonverbal behavior in others. Of the necessary oral communication skills, the most significant business communication need at the entry job level is small group communication skill.

Swenson (1980) surveyed a major section of American industry concerning communication skills and discovered that large and small group communication within the firms was considered the most significant aspect of business speech communication. Conflict arises in this area because it has been found that entry level employees generally bring to the job weak or nonexistent skills in group communication and a companion inability to listen to their immediate supervisors' suggestions and advice. We have devoted Chapter 9 to discussion of small group communication and the carryover effect of leadership and followership training to the general needs of business.

CONFLICT AREA 4: THE PROBLEM EMPLOYEE

There are numerous reasons why employees cause problems on the job. A few of them, previously noted, are

1. problems with management because employees are not properly informed of business decisions and therefore perceive threats to their job security
2. the coldness of an organization's structure, resulting in uncertainty and ambiguity about to whom one talks and to whom one complains about working conditions

Mariette Pathy Allen/Peter Arnold, Inc.

The location of action—a supervisor and employee getting along

3. a lack of an atmosphere in which supervisors and workers can share common problems and deal with issues in an open and free exchange of ideas and solutions

It is obvious that getting along on the job with your colleagues is a full-time task. Managing people involves daily change and conflict, and deciding what to do with a problem employee may consume as much of a working day as the work itself.

CONFLICT AREA 5: LEARNING TO DEAL WITH CONFLICTS

All four of the previously cited conflict areas lead to a final area of conflict on the job—an area in which effective communication skills play the significant role in conflict resolution. Short-range and long-range business goals require a clear and ever-present attack on conflict areas, so that every employee can learn to deal with both continuity and change and can learn to live with and learn from conflicts.

Sources indicate that one of every four workers is potentially emotionally disturbed, with problems sufficient to visibly disturb work (Swenson, 1980). We also know that supervisors and managers may unthinkingly put pressure on employees by setting production and quality standards too high. In addition, they sometimes fail to praise employees for good work and use scare tactics to threaten workers if the work is not up to the company's standards.

Although we hope it is not likely, you could become a problem supervisor or manager, joining others already on the job. If you preach too much, are stingy with information and praise, and generally abuse your communication authority, *you* are the problem and you need help. Organizational and personal goals for proper operation of a business, however, generally focus on choosing among several right ways to accomplish a common objective.

Organizations often try to insulate themselves from conflict because it might lead to downturns in productivity. Many businesses, for example, might hesitate to hire creative people because they fear these people will create conflict that will give the business serious problems sooner or later. We can safely assume that some types of conflict are bad because they destroy the fabric of the business. Not all conflict is destructive, however, for either the employee or the company. Conflict can be valuable for motivating action and solving problems. As an example, conflict within a work environment can help you learn to cope with that environment by allowing you to say what you think to your superiors. Coping with the work place is often a matter of "fight or flight." By developing skills in resolving problems with reason and patience, you also can learn to live with your colleagues and their needs to know, to tell, to direct, and to understand.

Conflicts also can provide a healthy restraint on goal aspirations. It has been our experience that one's goals are often more realistically trimmed to obtainable levels when all the goals shared by one's colleagues are discussed and efficiently channeled. Sometimes it takes an airing of plans and problems, even followed by heated discussion, before real progress is achieved. A good argument can have a very beneficial effect.

GETTING ALONG ON THE JOB

Finally, as part of our brief examination of conflict between labor and management, we offer a list of suggestions to aid in resolving personality clashes:

1. Only a functioning, open-channeled organization can settle conflicts that are halting or altering production or services. Even if you cannot change the situation personally, you can understand the problems.
2. The best organizational linking of the worker and the boss is for them to accept one another as they are. This may sound too simple, but it does work. It is important to focus on the interpersonal bonds you can establish; productive solutions to small group situations may follow as a natural result.
3. Often managers, supervisors, and other management people unconsciously cause conflicts with workers. One source of such conflict is regressive nonverbal habits that make human relations brittle and harsh. We will not discuss nonverbal behavior in great detail here, but you should be aware that your silent messages spread and multiply interpersonal conflicts well beyond your direct control.
4. The organizational chart is sometimes viewed as suppressive by employees who are attempting to send upward communications. The most desirable solution is to have autonomy within each department or unit. Most important is making the system work. There are no easy answers, but good communications and good relations can exist between employees and employer if both sides are willing to work together on the natural conflicts that arise each day.
5. It is important that you do not hide your feelings from your colleagues or subordinates when you are in low spirits. If

you do, those people will not come to you when they are feeling low. They will think that you cannot help them because you never seem to be down on yourself or others.

6. You should spend half of your work place time listening. No one person is directly responsible for communication policies in any business. You are in charge of your own communication environment, so, in Shakespeare's words, "Give every man thy ear, but few thy voice" (Hamlet I, iii, 65).

SUMMARY

In this chapter we have discussed five major areas of conflict, and we have suggested six responses to conflict situations. We have indicated a variety of measures to help you understand your role in the organizational environment. As we move into the skills chapters of *Let's Talk Business,* you should be more aware of and sensitive to the premise that effective daily communication patterns and meaningful human relationships are possible through conflict resolution. No one ever goes looking for conflict, but problems should lead to the growth of the individual and the company, not to their destruction.

EXERCISES

For this chapter, rather than posing a series of questions, we have provided three case studies. Each of these hypothetical cases is based on a real experience. Using the materials in Chapter 4, you can discuss each case in a small group setting, in open class, or in a written report.

Case studies 2 and 3 are particularly useful models for group discussion. To prepare for the discussion, you should draw up a list of communication strategies that seem most applicable to each case. After discussing the two Jones Sporting Goods, Inc., cases, you might have the impression that the employee must do much more personality adjustment than the manager or the company—and you might be right. These case studies focus on an understanding of your feelings about the daily strains and joys of a productive business career as you progress through phase I.

Case study 1: Conflict management—
the problem employee

Fred Wilkes, supervisor of ABC Company's tool and die shop, walked back to his desk with a frown on his face. "Gee," he thought, "who would ever have thought that Charlie would get to be such an old grouch? He's getting to be the biggest problem I've got."

Charlie Zales, who had come to the company just after the Vietnam War, was a skilled tool and die maker of the old school. Fred had considered himself lucky to be able to hire such a good workman. Charlie hadn't been around long, however, before it became evident that he had faults as an employee. He was crotchety and fussy. His tools had to be set up in just the right order. He couldn't work on rush jobs or jobs that required cutting corners. He obviously didn't approve of the men he worked with or their work habits.

Over the years, Fred had felt that Charlie's good points outweighed his petty gripes and complaints. In the last year or so, however, Charlie had become harder than ever to work with and to get along with. One day he'd complain about someone who had opened the windows and let in a draft. The next day he'd fuss about a change the engineering department had asked for that wasn't on the original print. Today, Charlie had said that the light was so poor it gave him a headache. (It was the same lighting that he had worked under for ten years.) He asked how Fred could expect him to work under these conditions.

As such complaining went on, day after day, Fred was losing his patience and his sympathy with Charlie. It seemed to Fred that, the more he tried to help Charlie, the more things Charlie could find that weren't right or were wrong. Moreover, Charlie's talents weren't as hard to do without as they once were. There were several younger tool and die makers who could do all his work and more now, and they were much easier to get along with.

Fred thought about the situation: "The next time Charlie gets out his crying towel, I'm going to turn a deaf ear to him. Or I'll just tell him what the situation is, and tell him just what I think."

What do you think of Fred's decision?

How do you think Charlie will react when Fred tells him what he thinks of him?

Why do you think Charlie has become so difficult?

What would you do if you were Fred?

**Case study 2: General manager,
Jones Sportings Goods, Inc.**

You are the general manager of Jones Sporting Goods, Inc., a new corporation in Smalltown. You have been employed for fifteen years at a sister plant of the firm in Ohio, starting as an office boy and working your way up through sales, purchasing, production, and on to management. You were general manager of the Ohio plant for three years before coming to Smalltown. No one in the corporation's system of plants knows more about the management of a plant than you. Last year, the home office in Chicago gave a testimonial dinner in your honor to show the company's appreciation for the fine job you have done and are doing.

You have received a memo from the home office that a new vice-president for plant personnel has been hired and that he is going to try to work on the downward and upward communication channels of the plant. Although such plans might look good on paper, you know that the strength of the corporation has always been its flexibility. The key to this flexibility has been management development and solid human relations in in-service training. New plant communication structures have tended to find a satisfactory level over time.

You are aware that, if this new policy takes effect, it not only will reduce the plant's flexibility but will signal an end to the normal process of learning to live with one another and to your stewardship as the general manager.

You are determined that the new vice-president will not enforce his policy. He probably means well, but he just doesn't understand the business as you do. You have the experience and the credibility with the corporation. You know that you will have to make your points quickly and decisively when you talk to him. He has to know who is the boss at this plant location. Your prestige with your subordinate managers rests on the outcome of this meeting.

Case study 3: Vice-president for plant personnel, Jones Sporting Goods, Inc.

You have just been hired as the chief plant supervisor of personnel for Jones Sporting Goods, Inc., a new corporation in Smalltown. Your title is vice-president for plant personnel. You have a Ph.D. in personnel management from the state university, you have headed several national advisory boards on plant management, and you have published a workbook for supervisors—an on-the-job communication training manual. You see improvement of the downward and upward communication channels of the new corporation as the best way to bring order out of chaos.

You have decided to have monthly meetings of all of the major units in the plant, to establish newsletters and suggestion boxes, to hold special lunch sessions for the plant workers and the management, and to initiate a number of other communication strategies to meet future needs and to nip current problems in the bud.

You have decided to put these policies into operation by visiting every person under your supervision, informing him or her of your plans, explaining the necessity of your master plan, and insisting on full cooperation. You know that you may meet stiff opposition, but you are the expert hired to handle the job, and you have been given the power to do it as you see fit. You are determined that you will not be sidetracked by minor objections; you are the only one who knows and understands the proved effectiveness of such a plan.

REFERENCES AND SUGGESTED READINGS

Herzberg, Frederick. 1968. "One More Time: How Do You Motivate Employees?" *Harvard Business Review* 46:53–62.
Kahan, Robert L., and Building, Elsie. 1964. *Power and Conflict.* New York: Basic Books.
Swenson, Dan H. 1980. "Relative Importance of Business Communication Skills for the Next Ten Years." *Journal of Business Communication* 17 (Winter):41–49.

Chapter 5

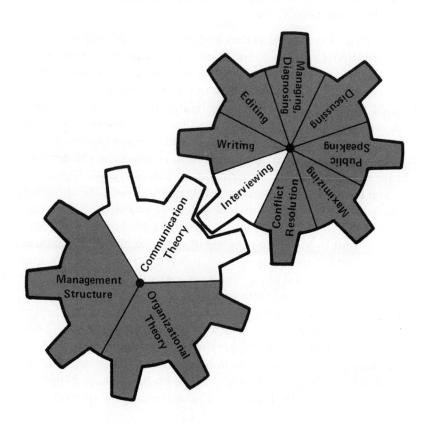

ON THE JOB: SKILLS IN INTERVIEWING

This chapter will provide you with the following:

1. an increased awareness of the use of interviews in business and organizations

2. an understanding of specific skills needed to conduct an interview or to participate in an interview

3. an understanding of specific procedures to follow in preparing for and participating in interviews

4. a knowledge of the basic structure of the interview situation

5. the ability to identify four broad types of interview situations

6. an understanding of the purpose, use, and special characteristics of the four interview types

7. the ability to plan an interview

8. the ability to conduct a good interview as an interviewer

9. the ability to participate effectively as an interviewee

The subject of interviewing is a broad one, and much has been written about it. Entire books are devoted to specialized forms of interviewing, such as interviewing for newspaper reporters, interviewing for welfare workers, interviewing for social science research, and, of course, interviewing for personnel managers in business. Our purpose in this chapter is to give you some major principles for the several types of interview situations that will be important to you in the business world.

Some writers have developed complex categories of interview types, such as the free interview, the area interview, the patterned interview, the nondirected interview, the probing interview, the stress interview, the group interview, and the board interview (Latham, 1964). Others have delineated such interviews as the appointment interview, the counseling interview, the work appraisal interview, the disciplinary interview, the exit interview, the information-seeking interview, and the persuasive interview (Lahiff, 1973).

Rather than focusing on interview situations and types, this chapter will discuss specific skills that are needed and procedures to be followed. After developing these general principles, we will touch briefly on four situational types: an initial employment interview, a supervisory interview, a performance appraisal interview, and a conflict resolution interview.

THE INTERVIEW STRUCTURE

Before we analyze the specific skills and procedures for interviews, or the four types and situations, we shall discuss the basic structure of most interview situations. A simple, three-point pattern applies to most interviews.

First is the period of *opening*. This phase, characterized by informal conversation, or small talk, is designed to reduce tension, to allow people to become acquainted or reacquainted, and to smooth the way for the more formal interview. Depending on the situation, this period can be very short, with such exchanges as

A gathering of information—the spirit of an interview

"How's it going today?" or "What's new?" or any of the many cliches we use to express interest in another person without expecting any particular or specific answers. In some situations, however, this phase can be rather lengthy—especially if the interviewer and interviewee are not well acquainted.

Second is a period of *substantive exchange*. This is the phase in which most of the actual business of the interview takes place. This portion is usually characterized by more structure, formality, and a degree of seriousness.

Third is a period of *closing*. In this phase, the interview is brought to a formal conclusion. This phase also usually involves some indication of the steps that will follow the interview.

Figure 5.1 indicates a general flow pattern for most interview situations. The direction and size of the arrow indicate the thrust of the interview between interview and interviewee.

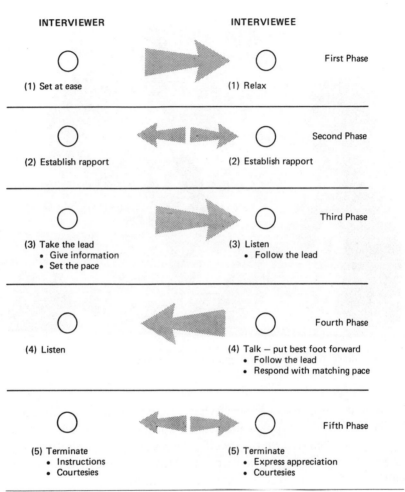

INTERVIEWER	INTERVIEWEE	
(1) Set at ease	(1) Relax	First Phase
(2) Establish rapport	(2) Establish rapport	Second Phase
(3) Take the lead • Give information • Set the pace	(3) Listen • Follow the lead	Third Phase
(4) Listen	(4) Talk — put best foot forward • Follow the lead • Respond with matching pace	Fourth Phase
(5) Terminate • Instructions • Courtesies	(5) Terminate • Express appreciation • Courtesies	Fifth Phase

FIGURE 5.1   Interview phases

INTERVIEWER SKILLS

The general skills that are helpful to the interviewer, regardless of the interviewing situation, can be briefly categorized into four characteristics: empathy, clarity, discernment, and fairness. Applying these skills in harmony can make you a more effective interviewer.

Empathy

It is important that the interviewer have a genuine feeling for broad aspects of the interview situation and for the person to be interviewed. An intense desire for a pleasant and productive interview is crucial. The tone set by the interviewer can have a significant impact on the mood and response of the interviewee and, therefore, on the ultimate success of the interview.

Clarity

The interviewer should be able to phrase concepts and questions clearly and concisely. It is poor practice for the interviewer to be verbose and rambling and to control too much of the interview time with presentation of personal accomplishments or personal interests. Clarity and conciseness should not be confused, however, with a curt or abrupt manner, which is clearly undesirable. The interviewer should phrase questions as simply as possible, to ease understanding and to enhance the situation for the interviewee, and should avoid stacking questions—giving one question at a time.

Discernment

The successful interviewer must have the ability to listen effectively and critically. Most interviews have a very specific purpose and should be structured so as to provide information that the interviewer is seeking. The successful interviewer must be capable of critical listening, successfully grasping and interpreting the pertinent information as it is received. Note taking should be kept to a minimum, so that the interviewee is not made uneasy by an indication that every utterance is a matter of permanent record.

Fairness

The successful interviewer must maintain strict control of the interviewing situation. In such a position of control, it is imperative that the interviewer be fair in dealing with the interview situation.

This fairness should be represented by such characteristics as lack of bias, consistency, and integrity. The interviewer should avoid leading, loaded, or similarly unfair questions.

INTERVIEWEE SKILLS

The interviewer is normally the person in control of the interview situation, but the interviewee also must possess certain skills for success in the interview situation. Although these skills must be adapted to the particular type of interview, the following types of skills are generally useful: cogenial attitude, analytical and organizational ability, direct communication, and confidence.

Congenial attitude

Each interview situation must be analyzed in its own setting regarding the type of behavior that would be appropriate. A congenial attitude should be the norm, however, for most interview situations. The interview should have a pleasant, positive, and helpful tone. A high-pressure, overly jovial presentation should be avoided, as should a nervous, quiet, reserved attitude.

Analytical and organizational ability

The interview situation demands that a person be capable of responding quickly to spontaneous questions. The interviewee should be careful to think before speaking. It is better to have a few seconds of silence while you analyze your thoughtful answer than to begin speaking before you have given the matter appropriate thought. This analytical and organizational ability requires that you continue thinking and organizing your answer while you begin speaking. Normally, a response to an interview question should follow some organized pattern, although it is well-accepted practice for additional thoughts to be added, even if they may seem out of sequence. Appropriate comments may be added with the use of such connecting phrases as "and I would also" or "I think another point would be."

Direct communication

Because most interview situations are structured in a short time frame, the substantive exchange portion of the interview should be characterized by straightforward, direct communication. The interviewee should respond as specifically, clearly, and concisely as possible to the question or subject under discussion. It is better to admit lack of knowledge or lack of certainty about an issue than to speak circuitously. Usually, the interviewee should not attempt to create an answer about an area in which he or she lacks knowledge or information. The interviewee might speak to the point by indicating lack of specific knowledge but referring to general information he or she might have on the subject.

As an example, if the interviewer asks if you have ever had any experience keeping books, you might answer: "Actually, Mr. Barton, I've never actually kept books, but during the two summers that I worked as a teller for First State Bank I learned a lot about balancing my daily log and being responsible for accounting for all monies handled. I feel that the experience I gained from the bank position has given me a sense of appreciation for the tremendous responsibility involved in keeping books and has made a definite contribution to my accounting education."

Confidence

The interviewee should be able to present a strong, positive self-concept throughout the interview. Because the interviewer will be in control of the interview situation, the interviewee needs to demonstrate personal strength through strong self-confidence. Although cockiness should be avoided, confidence should be demonstrated. The interviewee should avoid indications of lack of self-assurance—head hung down or failure to look at the interviewer directly, wringing of hands, fingering a paper or pen, drumming fingers on a desk top, clutching hands tightly—some of the visible evidence of nervousness or lack of self-confidence. Many interviewers look for these characteristics and make important value judgments on the basis of this evaluation criterion.

PROCEDURES FOR THE INTERVIEWER

Whatever the interview situation, there are certain preparatory procedures that the interviewer should take into consideration. These suggestions are intended as general guidelines to be adapted to the specific purpose and type of interview.

Organize

Be sure that the interview situation is well organized. Remember that, as the interviewer, you are in control of the situation and should have all arrangements properly established. Factors to consider include the setting where the interview will occur, the time allowed for it, and any materials that might be needed. In an employment interview, for example, if you have an advance copy of the applicant's resume, be sure you have it available and marked for any questionable points. If you plan to give the applicant information about your company, be sure to have the information packaged and ready to give.

Determine the purpose

Be certain that you have a clear understanding of the essential purpose of the interview. Your purpose may fit one of the four major categories presented in this chapter or it may have a special purpose. In any event, as the person in control of the interview, it is imperative that you have a clear understanding of what you hope to gain from the interview. After you have formulated a statement of the purpose, use this statement to develop some general questions.

Frame general questions

It is generally a good idea for the interviewer to have a set of basic, broad, general questions to use during the interview session. This procedure helps to assure that you accomplish your objectives and cover all important areas, and that the interview moves along on schedule. You should be careful, however, to keep the questions general and to make certain that there is room for spontaneous questions. Some flexibility is important so that you can adapt your questioning to the flow of the interview, based on the responses and interaction generated in the course of the interview. If any specific questions are needed, be prepared to ask these, too. In an employment interview, for example, you may have some very specific questions after a preliminary review of the applicant's resume, such as: "John, I notice you have moved from job to job with considerable frequency and that your longest time in a job was just over two years. Is there anything in particular that has caused this?"

Have needed materials available

You should determine whether you will need any informational material available during the interview. If you are going to use charts or graphs to make some general comments in the introductory portion of your interview session, for example, you should make certain that such charts or graphs are available and ready for your use. If you anticipate giving materials to the interviewee to peruse or take away for later review, be sure that you have them on hand and prepared for presentation. If you are going to use a checklist form to keep track of your interview and your reactions, be sure that the form is ready for you to use so that it will not be a problem for you as you enter the actual interview situation. (See Figure 5.2 for a sample checklist.)

Plan your closing

The closing of an interview can be an extremely important element, but it is often overlooked. Some interviews are brought to a close by a simple indication that the time has expired. Some interviewers save a crucial question for the very end. Others use this as a time to give a briefing about procedures, steps to follow, or other information on postinterview activities. If you plan your closing, you will not be caught in the awkward situation of making an abrupt ending. You will feel better about the interview and so will the interviewee. As an informed participant in the business com-

Opening	Check when completed
Introduction	_____
Informal conversation	_____
Clarification of purpose of interview	_____

Substantive Exchange

Basic information exchange	_____
Distribution of printed matter	_____
Interviewer's general questions	_____
Interviewer's specific questions	_____
Interviewee's questions	_____

Closing

Concluding instructions	_____
Review and summary of interview	_____
Concluding courtesies	_____

FIGURE 5.2   Sample interviewer checklist

munity, you should know the importance of closure and should use it effectively in the interview situation.

Follow up

In most interview situations, some type of brief written follow-up is helpful. A brief summary, a note expressing appreciation, or other comments can help produce an excellent feeling about an interview, regardless of the final outcome. The brief written follow-up helps ensure goodwill (McConnell, 1979).

PROCEDURES FOR THE INTERVIEWEE

Although the interview situation is primarily controlled by the interviewer, there are procedures that an interviewee should consider. A little bit of planning effort can go a long way toward making your interview a more successful experience.

If the interview is an initial employment interview, you will need to provide some type of personal data sheet or resume. Some companies have a form that they will want you to use, while others will ask you to submit a personal data sheet. To obtain an initial employment interview, you must usually submit an application letter, which is sent with the general-purpose personal data sheet. (Figure 5.3 is a sample of a general-purpose personal data sheet, and Figure 5.4 is a sample of an application letter.)

The following suggested procedures are intended as general guidelines to be adapted to specific interview situations.

PERSONAL DATA SHEET

Jill Ann Jones

PERSONAL AND FAMILY DATA   Picture

    Address: 1001 Stead Court, Apt. 1
            Crystal, CA 01234

    Date and Place of Birth: June 14, 1964; Terre Haute, IN

    Height: 5'6"   Weight: 125 lbs.   Health: Excellent

    Marital Status: Single   Hobbies and Sports: Jogging, tennis, reading

EDUCATION

    1982-86: Indiana University, Bloomington, IN—B.B.A (expected
      June 1986)
    1978-82: North High School, Terre Haute, IN—Diploma

continued

FIGURE 5.3   Sample general-purpose personal data sheet

ACADEMIC PREPARATION

Major: Marketing (27 semester hours)

Courses: Principles of Marketing, Retail Advertising, Advanced Marketing, Fundamentals of Advertising, Retailing, Research in Marketing, Marketing Campaigns, Psychology in Marketing, Principles of Sales

Other Business Courses: Accounting, 12 hours; Business Communications, 6 hours; Business Law, 6 hours; Finance, 6 hours; Statistics, 6 hours; Management, 3 hours

Grade Point Average: Major—3.5 of 4.0   Overall—3.1 of 4.0

HONORS AND ACTIVITIES

College: president of Phi Beta Lambda, first place in state PBL tournament (senior year), member of Pi Kappa Alpha, advertising sales staff for campus daily newspaper, member of Student Foundation

High School: Vice-president of Student Government, Junior Achievement, president of Future Business Leaders Club

BUSINESS EXPERIENCE

Part-time 1984-86: Teller, First State Bank, Bloomington, IN

Summers, 1983, 1984: Office Assistant, Mammoth Cave National Park, KY

Summer, 1982: Sales Assistant, Kelly Office Supply, Terre Haute, IN

REFERENCES

Mrs. Hazel Tree, Office Manager, Mammoth Cave National Park, KY 44110

Mrs. Susan Anthony, Head Teller, First State Bank, Bloomington, IN 47401

Dr. Dean Tooth, Professor of Marketing, Indiana University, Bloomington, IN 47401

FIGURE 5.3   Continued

1001 Hampden Court
Anytown, USA 09876
June 14, 1983

Ms. Judy Will
Personnel Officer
Wiregoods Products Corp.
Goodtown, USA 01234

Dear Ms. Will:

I read with interest your position announcement for a programmer analyst, and I am applying for the position. Enclosed you will find a copy of my resume, which outlines my personal background and experience.

My academic preparation in computer science and data processing has prepared me for a position as programmer analyst. In addition, you will note from my resume that I have had several work experiences during my college studies. In my sophomore and junior years I worked as a part-time assistant to one of the programmer analysts in the university's computer center. During my senior year I had a cooperative education business internship program with Eadon Corporation and served as an assistant to a programmer analyst with that firm.

If you need any additional information from me, I would be very pleased to respond to your request. I will look forward to hearing from you.

Sincerely,

David T. Hall

FIGURE 5.4   Sample application letter

Plan appropriate protocol

Before your appointment, consider the possible dynamics you will face as you enter the interview situation. Think of the role and status of the person who will be interviewing you, and consider the appropriate way to greet and to address him or her during the interview. Will you use Mr., Ms., Dr., or will you be on a first-name basis? You should also consider where the interview will take place and what type of dress and manner will be appropriate. Should you wear a suit or nice dress, or would more casual clothing be acceptable? Sensitivity to these issues can be extremely important during the opening portion of the interview in forming the basis for a successful substantive interview.

Know your subject

Whatever the main topic of the interview is, you should be certain that you are thoroughly familiar with any necessary information. The more you can avoid obscure references, and the more specific and informed you can appear, the greater success you will have in the interview.

If you are being interviewed regarding a personnel complaint you have made, for example, you should have specifics in mind. It is not enough to say, "Mary and I just can't get along together!" or "I don't know what it is, but he really bothers me." Be specific and say, for example, "Mary uses my equipment without asking me, she rummages through my desk when I'm away, and she is always telling me her personal problems until it makes me practically sick."

If you are having an employment interview for a marketing job at a trucking firm, for example, try to obtain as much information as possible about the trucking industry—to add to your academic training in marketing.

Construct possible questions

It may be helpful for you to attempt to analyze the interview situation and compile some possible general questions that you might be required to answer. This can give you some preinterview practice in dealing with potential questions. Sometimes you may find it useful to construct a list of questions that you would like to answer. For advance preparation, pretend that you are the interviewer. Sometimes you can weave into the actual interview some points of information that you have determined in advance would be particularly helpful for you to share.

For some interview situations, you may also wish to construct a list of questions you would like to ask the interviewer if the opportunity is provided. In an employment interview, for example, you might list questions about such matters as the working hours, the fringe benefits, the mood of the office, the opportunities for promotion, and the vacation program. It is better to have these items developed through preplanning than to be caught in the actual situation and found not thoroughly prepared.

Plan your conclusion

Although you will want to relate your specific closing to the flow of the interview, you should anticipate the types of comments that would be appropriate at the conclusion of the interview. Keep in mind your own status and that of the interviewer, as well as the subject of the interview, so that your concluding remarks will be appropriate as you respond to the interviewer's closure. You might conclude with a statement such as, "I really have appreciated this chance to visit with you" or "Thank you for sharing this time with me" and "I'll be looking forward to hearing from you."

Follow up

An interviewee should usually send a brief written follow-up to an interviewer. An expression of appreciation, a brief summary, or other comments may be appropriate. A thoughtful written follow-up can engender much goodwill. (Figure 5.5 presents a sample letter for a job interview follow-up.)

1001 Hampden Court
Anytown, USA 09876
June 14, 1983

Ms. Judy Will
Personnel Officer
Wiregoods Products Corp.
Goodtown, USA 01234

Dear Ms. Will:

Please accept my sincere appreciation for your cordial hospitality during my recent employment interview. I learned a great deal about your firm and the position of programmer analyst. The information covered in my visit and interview confirmed my feeling that it would be great to work for Wiregoods Products.

If you need any additional information from me, I would be very pleased to respond to your request. I will look forward to hearing from you.

Sincerely,

David T. Hall

FIGURE 5.5   Sample interview follow-up letter

INTERVIEW TYPES

As mentioned earlier, many writers have developed elaborate schemes and definitions of interview types and situations. In this chapter, we deal with four basic, broadly defined interview types: an initial employment interview, a supervisory interview, a performance appraisal interview, and a conflict resolution interview. The interview skills and procedures discussed earlier are adaptable to all of these situations. The following discussion is designed to increase your awareness of these four types and to describe briefly their purposes, uses, and major characteristics.

Initial employment interview

For many of you, the job interview may be foremost in your mind. We will therefore give more attention to this type of interview than to the other types. When Americans speak of a job interview, they usually are referring to the initial employment interview in which a prospective employee is interviewed as a way of determining suitability for employment by a firm or organization. Such interviews are conducted in many ways and with a variety of interview styles and techniques. The job interview may consist of a single interview or a series of interviews. It may involve one session and an immediate employment decision or multiple sessions, lasting for several hours, days, or even weeks, with a decision some time after the final interview. In this section we will examine three interview formats used in making employment decisions. In addition to the three formats described here, there are other formats and combinations of formats.

Information-sharing format This format least benefits both employer and prospective employee. One purpose of the information-sharing format is to assist the prospective employee in completing an application form. Normally, organizations that use this procedure require that the applicant complete a lengthy, detailed written form that sometimes requires rather obscure data. The interviewer in this setting is usually a low-ranking officer who performs a clerk-type function in making sure that the applicant understands and completes each question on an application form.

In an information-sharing interview, the interviewer may give you a written application form to complete. After you complete the form and return it, the interviewer may ask you to clarify some answers, saying, for example, "Mary, I notice you left the space by 'description of health' blank. How would you describe your current health?" or "Mary, I see you can type at 80 words per minute. Do you enjoy typing?" During such a questioning process, the interviewer will make additional notes to consider in determining how to dispose of the application.

Such an interview is not very satisfying for the applicant, since there is little if any opportunity to present unique personal qualities or attributes. Since the interviewer in such a situation often is not in a position to make an employment decision, the interviewee may be concerned that the interview will not provide an accurate evaluation of strengths and special personal traits and that it will not have a direct effect on the employment decision. Sometimes the information-sharing interview is a first step, allowing an initial screening of applicants before a decision to give serious consideration to an applicant.

Evaluative format   The evaluative interview is a serious method that seeks to determine competence for the position through explicitly directed questioning. This format, sometimes referred to as a probing interview, usually operates from a specific set of questions that have been prepared to determine your qualification for the job. In this type of interview, the questioner often will begin a general topic with a broad question, such as, "How did you become interested in the field of accounting?" Following up on the topic through a series of questions, the interviewer probably will ask a knowledgeable question to test your competence, such as, "Are you familiar with process costing procedures?" The interviewer also probably will ask you some judgment questions, such as, "What do you see as the most critical issues in accounting during the next decade?"

Through this intensive questioning, the interviewer adds information to the candidate's resume, makes judgments about the candidate's personal qualities, and assesses intellectual and critical abilities of the applicant. Although most of the judgments are highly subjective, the questioner usually operates from a set plan of detailed questions that are designed to probe objective knowledge as well as subjective areas of critical thinking and intellectual judgment.

Although much job interviewing is done on a strictly one-on-one basis, with an interviewer and an interviewee, various group settings are also used. The different types of interviews sometime require different formats. The information-sharing format is probably most often conducted in a one-on-one setting. The information obtained is straightforward, with less room for interpretation. As the interview purpose moves away from recording factual information to making evaluative judgments, however, it is often beneficial to use several interviewers in a group setting—according to the adage that two heads are better than one.

When a group conducts an interview, the interviewee may feel more relaxed. If the group seems to pounce on the individual, however, then the group setting obviously can intensify anxiety for the job applicant. Group interviews should be designed in advance so that all group members have information about the interviewee and a general idea of the questions to be asked and the directional flow of the discussion. Group members may keep individual checklists or notes, and they should meet after the candidate has left to share their evaluations and judgments.

In general, if judgment decisions need to be made as a result of the interview, it is wise to consider using the group approach. If the purpose of the interview is to gather facts, it is better to use a single interviewer.

Casual format Another form of interviewing prospective employees uses an informal, nondirective, or casual approach. In this format, the interview may be held in an office, at a luncheon, or in an informal reception situation. The primary purpose of the casual format interview is to get a feel for the interviewee's success in interpersonal relationship skills, with only limited interest in specific job-related skills. This type of interview, conducted in a nonthreatening environment, produces a relaxed mood for sharing views on job-related matters and other general areas.

The casual format interview might begin with an open question, such as, "John, suppose you begin by just telling a little bit about yourself—where you are from, your family background, your education, your goals for the future." Such a question provides the interviewee with an opportunity to present personal, biographical information selectively—picking those aspects deemed most appropriate. In such a setting, the candidate can also give emphasis to and embellish accomplishments and attributes that present himself or herself in the best possible way.

Occasionally, the casual interview setting may be used to determine a candidate's sociability, etiquette, or other such quali-ties. The casual interview may especially be used if the job applied for requires special adeptness with social protocol. In such a set-ting, the interviewee may be evaluated on dress, social courtesies, social conversational ability, and breadth of interest in literature, the arts, sports, or other areas. The casual interview employed in this way is normally used in conjunction with other more serious and formal interviews that are directly related to the job.

Supervisory interview

The purpose of a supervisory interview is to provide direct com-munication between a supervisor and a subordinate on a special issue. This type of interview is used for a variety of purposes, such as to clarify a working relationship, to solve a specific work-related problem, or to explore job issues. A special characteristic of this type of interview is that the parties involved are usually well known to each other; thus, the initial relationship-building portion of the interview frequently may be shortened or omitted.

Performance appraisal interview

The purpose of a performance appraisal interview is to provide a specific evaluation of an employee's performance. It is used by many companies and organizations in many areas, including its use as a basis for salary adjustment, promotion, and setting pro-fessional development and job-related goals. Several character-istics of this type of interview can be identified. Most companies and organizations have a very structured program of employee evaluation, and the interview between the employee and the em-ployee's supervisor is a normal part of the evaluation process. The interview typically follows a structured pattern, based on the in-dividual organization's forms for recording the evaluation. An-other characteristic of this type of interview is the high degree of tension and anxiety that accompanies an evaluation discussion. With this in mind, the interviewer should make every effort to reduce tension and to be supportive and positive in conducting the interview.

Conflict resolution interview

The purpose of a conflict resolution interview is to attempt to resolve a specific conflict. It is used in a variety of settings in business organizations, including efforts between individual employees, between supervisor and subordinate, and between the organization and external clients.

Several characteristics identify the conflict resolution interview. It usually involves a high degree of tension and a need to make every effort to reduce that tension. There is a strong need for delineating the issues and pinpointing the problem areas and issues that must be resolved to diminish the conflict. There is also a strong need to establish a sense of fairness and openness between the conflicting parties. Every effort should be made to keep heads cool, to hear both sides fully, and to encourage a conciliatory give-and-take attitude so that a compromise consensus can be achieved.

SUMMARY

In this chapter, specific skills were identified for both the interviewer and the interviewee. The chapter also outlined procedures to be followed and adapted to most interview situations. The basic interview structure was identified as a simple three-point system of opening, substantive exchange, and closing. Interview types and situations were classified broadly into four categories: the initial employment interview, the supervisory interview, the performance appraisal interview, and the conflict resolution interview. The purpose, use, and special characteristics of each type were briefly described.

EXERCISES

1. Divide the class into groups of approximately five students each. Each group should be given the assignment of conducting an interview.
   a. Group instructions: Each group should select one person to serve as the interviewer and one person to serve as the interviewee; all other members of the group should serve as

observers. The group should select the type of interview to be done. Beginning students should be encouraged to use the initial employment interview type. The group should select a case study situation and develop information on the roles to be played by the interviewer and the interviewee.

b. Instructions for the interviewer:
   (1) Organize preparations for the interview.
   (2) Develop some general questions to use in the interview.
   (3) Have necessary materials available and ready to use.
   (4) Write out a plan for setting the interviewee at ease.
   (5) Write out a plan for closing the interview.
   (6) Write a follow-up letter to the interviewee.

c. Instructions for the interviewee:
   (1) Write a resume appropriate to the role you are playing.
   (2) Plan your initial protocol.
   (3) Know your subject.
   (4) Prepare some possible questions.
   (5) Write out a plan for your closing.
   (6) Write a follow-up letter to the interviewer.

d. Instructions for observers:
   (1) Use the Observer Checklist (Figure 5.6) to identify the steps being followed throughout the interview.
   (2) Use the Observer Checklist to make quality judgments about the interviewer and the interviewee.
   (3) Write a paper evaluating the interview.

2. Prepare a resume that you could use if you were applying for employment today.

3. Prepare a letter of application to accompany your resume. Apply to a company and position of your choice.

4. Write a paper evaluating the interview in the Barton Company case study.
   a. Label the type of interview.
   b. Evaluate Mr. Beltz's skills as an interviewer in the categories of empathy, clarity, discernment, and fairness.
   c. Evaluate Buddy's skills as an interviewee in the categories of congenial attitude, analytical ability, directness, and confidence.

OBSERVER CHECKLIST
for classroom observation of an interview

Skill	Interviewer Rate from 1 to 5 (1=poor; 5=excellent)	Interviewee Rate from 1 to 5 (1=poor; 5=excellent)
Opening 1. Was the student prepared?		
2. Was the student at ease?		
3. Did the student establish rapport?		
Substantive 4. Did the student give appropriate information?		
5. Did the student follow the lead of the other?		
6. Did the student display good listening?		
Closing 7. Did the student give instructions?		
8. Did the student express appreciation?		
9. Did the student show courtesies?		
Interviewer only 10. Empathy		
11. Clarity		
12. Discernment		
13. Fairness		
Interviewee only 14. Congenial attitude		
15. Analytical ability		
16. Directness		
17. Confidence		
TOTAL POINTS		

FIGURE 5.6   Observer checklist for classroom observation of an interview

Case study: The Barton Company

Buddy Boone was hired about six months ago as an order completion clerk. His supervisor was John Beltz, supervisor of the finished products/storeroom area. Mr. Beltz had observed Buddy
carefully over his first few months of work and had felt very good
about the progress of this young man as an outstanding addition
to his group of employees. Over the past four or five weeks, however, Mr. Beltz has observed a considerable change in Buddy's
behavior. Buddy has begun to miss work, to arrive late, and to fail
to complete orders properly, and he has demonstrated resentment
and belligerence when any suggestions for improvement have
been offered to him. Last week Buddy received a specific reprimand for excessive tardiness and for taking unauthorized leave
from the storeroom area. Although his behavior improved for a
couple of days, Buddy has returned to his poor work habits. Mr.
Beltz has decided that he must have a meeting with Buddy.

BELTZ: Buddy, I have been very concerned about some of the
changes that have been occurring in your behavior over
the last month or so. I want you to know that I felt very
good about your work when you first came to me. In fact, I
bragged about you to the other supervisors and had been
planning to recommend you for a pay adjustment. Candidly, however, I must tell you that your work has
deteriorated very rapidly and we are going to have to do
something to get you to straighten up or I may have to let
you go.

BUDDY: Well, that is pretty severe, Mr. Beltz. I sure have been having my troubles the last few weeks, but I am sure my performance has not been as bad as you are making it out.

BELTZ: It's no use trying to hide it, Buddy. I have been hinting at
the seriousness of your problems and you just don't seem
to respond.

BUDDY: Well, nobody's perfect, you know.

BELTZ: Maybe nobody is perfect, but you certainly were being an
excellent employee when you first came to my area and I
can tell you for sure that your performance has gone
down, down, down these past few weeks.

BUDDY: Well, I am willing to try harder.

BELTZ: That's what you have been telling me, Buddy, but it just hasn't been working. I thought that reprimand would change things, and it did, but that change only lasted for a day or two. You are right back in the same bad habits again.

BUDDY: Well, I really thought I had done quite a bit better since we had our last meeting about this.

BELTZ: Things did improve for a day or two, but, like I said, you just didn't stick. Something has to be done to make sure that you understand how serious this is.

BUDDY: Oh, I do, I do, and I mean to do better.

BELTZ: Buddy, I understand that you are not attending your evening classes over at the Vo-Tech school.

BUDDY: What—where did you hear that?

BELTZ: Oh, that is just what I learned, and I thought it fit right into this crazy pattern you have been following here at work lately.

BUDDY: Well, there is nothing to that. I have been attending my classes at the Vo-Tech school regularly.

BELTZ: One of my friends over at the school advised me the other day that you had quit coming to classes.

BUDDY: Well, I guess maybe you are kind of right. I have been having a lot of problems, as I was saying, and it has been tough going to school.

BELTZ: Well, I would like to know why you are not going to school. Is there anything I can do to help? You know you have a good mind and you could really make something of yourself if you can get this extra training.

BUDDY: Ah, it is no big deal. I mean, school is all right and I know I need it, but, well, I just haven't been able to make it to all of my classes.

BELTZ: It does seem to me like something has been bothering you, Buddy.

BUDDY: Bother me, oh no, it is nothing like that.

BELTZ: Honestly, Buddy, I am here to help you. Like I was telling you, I really did appreciate the great job you did for me when you first came to work here. I believe in you and I want to help you. You can trust me. Just tell me what it is that is bothering you so I can help you.

BUDDY: No, there is nothing the matter, nothing at all. I don't know why you would think there is something bothering me.

BELTZ: Well, let me put it to you just as clearly as I can. Your work when you started in my area was excellent. Your work has gone down, down, down. You absolutely must improve. You can do it. I know you can do it. You know you can do it.

BUDDY: Yes, I know I can do it and I intend to do it.

BELTZ: Well, that is all I have to say. I am going to be watching, Buddy, and if your work does not improve, I am going to have to let you go. That's just all there is to it. It is as plain and simple as that.

As the meeting broke up, Mr. Beltz was not at all sure that he had made any progress with Buddy. He worried that somehow his comments did not seem to be accepted. He wanted to help, but it seemed that Buddy wanted no help. Mr. Beltz determined that he would have to watch Buddy carefully to make certain that his work did improve, or he would have to recommend his termination.

REFERENCES AND SUGGESTED READINGS

Balinsky, Benjamin, and Burger, Ruth. 1959. *The Executive Interview.* New York: Harper & Brothers.

Lahiff, James M. 1973. "Interviewing for Results." In Richard C. Huseman, Cal M. Logue, and Dwight L. Freshley, eds., *Readings in Interpersonal and Organizational Communication,* 2nd ed., pp. 332-353. Boston: Holbrook Press.

Latham, James L. 1964. *Human Relations in Business.* Columbus, Ohio: Charles E. Merrill.

McConnell, Charles R. 1979. "Tips on Interviewing." *Management Digest* (February), p. 10.

Chapter 6

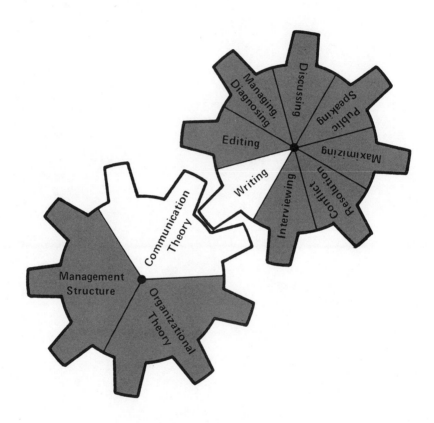

"Do This"
SKILLS IN WRITING

This chapter will provide you with the following:

1. an increased awareness of the importance of writing in a business career

2. the ability to identify the unique distinguishing characteristics of written and oral communications

3. the ability identify the basic characteristics of good business writing

4. an understanding of the who, what, and why of business memoranda, reports, and letters

5. the ability to produce appropriate business memos

6. the ability to produce appropriate business letters

7. the ability to produce appropriate business reports

Business leaders are increasingly viewed by society as sophisticated and highly educated people. Promotion of family members through closely held corporations or businesses just because they are family seems to be less frequent. Additional importance is being placed by all businesses and industries on appropriate educational background, preparation, and training. One of the marks of an educated person is the ability to communicate orally and in writing in an appropriate and effective manner. This chapter will assist you with some of the basic writing skills that are important in business, industry, and organizational managerial positions.

Although much of your communicating in business will be oral, you certainly will be required to produce numerous written documents. Later chapters in this book deal with oral communication in group situations and in informal public speaking situations. This chapter deals with the specific writing responsibilities you may have as a leader in business.

WRITING OR SPEAKING: WHAT'S THE DIFFERENCE?

We must clarify some of the differences between writing and speaking so that you can be aware of these special points as we get into the details of writing for business.

First, the audience in a writing situation is more general than the audience in a speaking situation. Writing to Mr. Jones generally is less direct than picking up the phone and talking to Mr. Jones or going down the hall to talk to him face-to-face. Normally, the spoken word is directed in a very particular setting and is not recorded for vast distribution, for the hearing of others not present, or as part of a permanent record. The written word, whether in a letter, memorandum, report, or other form, may be designed for a specialized audience, but it usually has an element of permanency that does not accompany the spoken word. Because a written document can be reviewed by many people, its audience is considered to be more general than that for a speaking situation.

Second, the mode of communication varies. In writing, the recipient of the written communication receives the information by reading it. Thus, writing has a special set of descriptive devices that accentuate the written word. Depending on the style of reading—intensive, casual, or spot-reading—reading places limitations on the writer. Speaking relies on listening and, therefore, has its own set of descriptive devices used for inflection in meaning. Because the speaker relies on the listener, who in most cases has only one opportunity to review the communication, the speaker must be more direct.

Third, the scope of the two modes varies. Written communication typically involves much more detail. It certainly is possible to transmit more detail accurately in written communication. In the spoken situation, less detail is involved because of the method of transmittal. The amount of detail that occurs in oral communication is directly proportional to the ease of understanding on first hearing, since it cannot be perused and the listener cannot skip to various portions of the communication to pick out a topic sentence.

Fourth, the method of reception is very different. Because of the permanency of a written communication, the writer can have the message reviewed with multiple chances for comprehension by the reader. The speaker, however, normally has only one opportunity to communicate successfully, since the listener will not be able to review the speaker's comments on multiple occasions.

CHARACTERISTICS OF GOOD
BUSINESS WRITING

Good business writing should be clear, concise, organized, appropriate, and examined. As we discuss the various types of writing that you may be required to do in the business world, you will see a need for skills in each of these areas.

Clarity

Good business writing requires that you state exactly what you mean to say. The use of big words, ambiguous terms, or overly

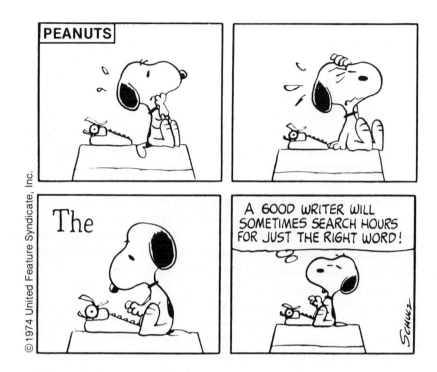

technical language usually should be avoided. Speak with words
that are as precisely chosen as possible.

Conciseness

Business leaders typically are extremely active, on-the-go people.
They are not interested in or impressed with verbosity or rambling thoughts. They prefer short, precise, almost choppy statements that go directly to the heart of issues.

Organization

Successful businesses usually have structure and organization in
their operations. People involved in business appreciate organizational structure and normally respond better to communications
that are highly organized and tightly structured. Excellent

organization and structure improve the immediate grasp of the communication and enhance recall.

Appropriateness

Business leaders expect language choice to be appropriate for the communication setting. The use of technical language, for example, should be determined by an evaluation of its appropriateness.

Examination

A good business writer will examine carefully what has been written. Using several minutes of your time to review your written

Effective writing is a premium communication skill in business

Ellis Herwig/Stock, Boston, Inc.

communication carefully can prove extremely beneficial in reducing errors and in reducing potential embarrassment about misstatements. Take a few moments to make sure that your written communication is correct, as you intended it, by examining it before it is sent.

TYPES OF BUSINESS WRITING: MEMORANDA, REPORTS, AND LETTERS

Although there are numerous classification schemes we could use for delineating various types of writing that business leaders might be engaged in, we believe that the three main headings of memoranda, reports, and letters provide an adequate structure in which to consider the types of writing used in the business world.

Memorandum formats

The memorandum is a much used, misused, and abused form of communication in all organizations and businesses. Memoranda usually are intended to be used primarily within an organization or business. As a form of internal communication, they have identifiable characteristics. Special skills in memo writing are outlined in this section to help make you a more effective business leader.

Memoranda can be either formal or informal communications. Formal memoranda, which are used to make a statement for the record, are therefore usually characterized by technical language, a nonpersonal tone, and a high degree of accuracy of information transmitted. Informal memoranda resemble face-to-face oral communications. They are typically characterized by nontechnical language and a high degree of personal reference, with the use of words that convey warm and personal feelings. Figures 6.1 through 6.3 reflect three styles of memoranda, ranging from very formal (Figure 6.1) to very informal (Figure 6.3).

Most organizations and companies have their own memoranda formats and encourage their use because it brings uniformity to company operations and enhances the communication

XYZ CORPORATION

1234 Industrial Boulevard

Anytown, USA 98765

Memorandum to: John Doan, Director of Contract Sales

From: Michael P. Zornigan, Vice President for Sales and Marketing

Date: November 12, 1983

Subject: Request for one additional sales position

I have carefully reviewed the material which you recently sent me concerning your possible need for an additional sales position. I must say that I found your views very interesting. I requested an independent review of this need by our personnel office and they concurred with my opinion that the current sales force is sufficient and therefore there is insufficient need for this additional position at this time.

Although it may be difficult for you to accept this, I hope you will understand. Please feel free to call me anytime if you have a question which you feel needs my attention.

FIGURE 6.1   Sample memorandum—formal

flow by giving a point of reference and an indication of a file heading. A typical memorandum format is shown in Figure 6.4.

Memoranda: Who, what, why?

Who   Since memoranda are used primarily for internal communications, you usually will be somewhat familiar with the precise audience for whom the memorandum is intended. Be sure to consider any special adaptations that should be made in the body of the memorandum to adapt it to the primary recipient of the

XYZ CORPORATION

1234 Industrial Boulevard

Anytown, USA 98765

Memorandum to: John Doan, Director of Contract Sales

From: Michael P. Zornigan, Vice President for Sales and Marketing

Date: November 12, 1983

Subject: Request for one additional sales position

The purpose of this memorandum is to officially advise you that I am
not approving your request of November 7, 1983, for an additional sales
representative position.

I am confident you and your staff will continue to do an outstanding
sales job.

FIGURE 6.2   Sample memorandum—less formal

XYZ CORPORATION

1234 Industrial Boulevard

Anytown, USA 98765

Memorandum to: John Doan, Director of Contract Sales

From: Michael P. Zornigan, Vice President for Sales and Marketing

Date: November 12, 1983

Subject: Request for one additional sales position

John, I really hate to have to tell you this but I am not able to approve
your request for an additional sales representative position. I know you
feel you have a very definite need, but I can't give you another position
without some additional staff in other areas.

So, John, although I'd love to give you this position, I hope you'll
understand.

FIGURE 6.3   Sample memorandum—informal

TOURO COLLEGE LIBRARY

MEMORANDUM

TO: REFERENCE NO.:

FROM: FILE NO.:

DATE:

SUBJECT:

_____

_____

_____

_____

_____

_____

_____

_____

COPIES TO:

_____

FIGURE 6.4   Memorandum format

communication. Decisions concerning the use of technical language and the degree of formality or informality should reflect your knowledge about the primary recipient.

What   The basic substance of the memorandum is crucial. Be sure that you know the subject thoroughly so that your knowledge is evidenced in the best possible way throughout the communication. Be certain to include all required information and to exclude trivial or unimportant information.

Why   The purpose of a memorandum is often stated in the first or second sentence. Occasionally, however, the ultimate purpose of

TOURO COLLEGE LIBRARY

the memorandum may remain unclear until some of the factual information is presented, in which case the memorandum may conclude with "Therefore, ..." In either case, be certain that the purpose of the memorandum is stated explicitly.

Businesses sometimes use memoranda to communicate information from the corporate or organizational leadership through the ranks to various other organizational officers. Although most of us are aware that passing information by word of mouth from one person to another person to still another subjects the information to distortion and sometimes gross miscommunication, we may not realize that some miscommunication can occur even when the information appears in writing. Figure 6.5, an example of a series of memoranda used to communicate very specific infor-

MEMORANDUM

FROM: Warden

TO: Associate Warden

Tomorrow evening at approximately 8:00 p.m., Halley's Comet will be visible in the area, an event which occurs only once every 75 years. Have the men file out in the yard area in white T-shirts and I will explain this rare phenomenon to them. In case of rain, we will not be able to see anything, so assemble the men in the theater and I will show films of it.

MEMORANDUM

FROM: Associate Warden

TO: Assistant Warden

By order of the Warden, tomorrow at 8:00 p.m. Halley's Comet will appear above the yard area. If it rains, fall the men out in T-shirts; then march them to the theater where the rare phenomenon will take place, something which occurs only once every 75 years.

continued

FIGURE 6.5   Sample series of memoranda

MEMORANDUM

FROM: Assistant Warden

TO: Shift Supervisor

By order of the Warden, in T-shirts at 8:00 p.m. tomorrow evening, the phenomenal Halley's Comet will appear in the theater. In case of rain in the yard area, the Warden will give another order, something which occurs once every 75 years.

MEMORANDUM

FROM: Shift Supervisor

TO: Division Cell Manager

Tomorrow at 8:00 p.m. the Warden will appear in the theater with the phenomenal Halley Comet which happens every 75 years. If it rains, the Warden will order Comet into the yard area in his white T-shirt.

MEMORANDUM

FROM: Division Cell Manager

TO: Cell Guard

When it rains tomorrow at 8:00 p.m., the phenomenal 75-year-old officer Halley accompanied by the Warden, will drive his Comet through the Yard Office to the theater in his white T-shirt.

FIGURE 6.5   Continued

mation, demonstrates how information can be distorted as it passes from supervisor to subordinate. Let this example be a warning to you that you cannot depend on having memorandum information interpreted and redistributed accurately. When a memorandum is being used to communicate such information, it is best for one person to write a memorandum that is then distributed to all necessary parties.

Report formats

The report is a written communication used heavily in businesses and organizations as a formal summary statement in response to a specific request. Requests for reports may require data collection, investigation, analysis, or other skills. Requests for reports should be as specific as possible, enabling the report writer to address the request very precisely. The format for reports is often dictated by company policy. Figure 6.6 is an example of a general format that might be used.

Reports: Who, what, why?

Who When you begin making plans for writing a report, consider carefully the audience that is to receive the report. Be sure that you know the background and preferences of the audience and the type of information and other related data that the audience would need, require, or desire. It is important that you use a writing style that is appropriate to the audience so that the information can be successfully transmitted and received. An analysis of the audience will assist you, for example, in determining the extent to which technical language can be used. Such analysis might also be crucial in determining the extent to which visual aids should be used as a part of the report. In all cases, as the report writer, you should remember that the report is prepared for people, so keep your writing lively and conducive to being read.

What The successful report writer must know and understand the subject thoroughly. Reports usually are somewhat formal documents designed for the transmission of detailed and often sophisticated information; therefore, the completeness of information is crucial for a successful report. Data in reports typically include substantial factual information and numerous figures and statistics. In presenting such information, it is often helpful to use charts, models, and other visually descriptive formats. Choose visual aids wisely, and avoid overusing them.

Why A report should state its purpose clearly to ensure proper communication between the report preparer and the report

Report Page 1

Report on _____

_____

_____

Prepared by

_____
Name

_____
Department

_____
Division-branch

_____
Company

Date, Year

FIGURE 6.6   Report format

Report Page 2

Summary: _____

_____

_____

_____

Recommendations:

1. _____

2. _____

3. _____

Discussion:

1. _____

_____

_____

2. _____

_____

_____

3. _____

_____

_____

FIGURE 6.6   Continued

© 1979 King Features Syndicate, Inc.

© 1979 King Features Syndicate, Inc. World rights reserved

reader. Before writing the report, the report preparer should determine if the purpose of the report is merely to distribute information or to present data on which a decision will be based. A report preparer should also determine if the report will be for temporary purposes or will be part of a permanent file, if it will be primarily for technical experts or for consumption by lay persons, and if it will be for individuals within or outside the organization. A clear understanding of these issues prior to preparation will assist the report preparer in a more effective presentation.

Letter formats

Business letters are an important part of the written communication used by business leaders. Your ability to communicate effectively through appropriate business letters will be an important skill. Business letters are required for a variety of purposes, such as to confirm a sales appointment, to make a bid, to confirm a sale, to announce a demonstration meeting for a product, to confirm a sale order, to answer an inquiry, and so on.

There are numerous formats for business letters, and they are constantly changing. The format of business letters may be dictated by company or organizational policy. Figure 6.7 is a sample of an appropriate business letter. The format and layout of this sample letter is not as important as the who, what, and why contained in it. Whatever the purpose or type of letter, you should consider the following points as aids in constructing successful business letters.

Letters: Who, what, why?

Who   Be sure to consider the personal characteristics of the individual who is to receive the letter. Whether the recipient will be a customer or client, a prospective customer, a supplier, or some other individual, that person will have an individual perspective and point of view. Frame your letter on a personal basis, keeping in mind your specific knowledge about the person to whom you are writing.

XYZ CORPORATION
1234 Industrial Boulevard
Anywhere, USA 98765

March 21, 1983

Mr. J. T. Jimmison
Vice President for Manufacturing
Trans-Tram Company
P. O. Box 555
Timbucktoo, USA 01234

Dear Mr. Jimmison:

I certainly enjoyed meeting you this past week. It's good to know another believer in the primacy of equipment reliability.

Your interest in our specially designed flow valve was gratifying. As I promised you during our meeting last week, I am sending enclosed with this letter a complete specification sheet for our AZ200 flow valve. This should provide you with the necessary information you requested. As you will see from these specifications, our product is made with the finest materials and is tuned to the most exacting specifications.

The current price for the AZ200 flow valve is $1,280 each or $1,200 in groups of 3 or more. This price quote is effective for 30 days, so just make certain your order is postmarked before April 21, 1983, to receive this special price.

J. T., our AZ200 flow valve has been proven extremely reliable. I know it would serve you well. Please call if you have unanswered questions or if I can be of assistance in other ways. We are grateful for the past business of your firm and we look forward to working with you in the future.

Sincerely,

William T. Dogood
Industrial Sales Representative

WTD:mac

Enclosure

FIGURE 6.7   Sample business letter

What In business organizations, it is important that you demonstrate your expertise. You must know your product thoroughly and be completely sold on it yourself if you are to be effective with others. In a business letter, it is important that you demonstrate thorough knowledge of the matter under discussion and that you deal with all items of business that must be covered. Remember that you represent your organization as well as yourself, so do your best work.

Why Every business letter must have a purpose. Make certain that you are clear and forthright about the purpose for the communication. In a business letter, expression of the purpose often will take the form of a phrase beginning "Therefore, . . ." In all cases, be sure that you state the purpose explicitly to avoid misunderstanding and miscommunication.

SUMMARY

This chapter has stressed the importance of good writing skills for a successful career in business. The differences between written and oral communication were identified to help you sharpen your writing skills specifically. The characteristics of good writing, identified as clarity, conciseness, organization, and appropriateness, were examined. Three major types of business writing were discussed: memoranda, reports, and letters. For each type special characteristics were identified, and suggestions and sample models were provided.

EXERCISES

1. Write a business memorandum on one of the following topics:
   a. to your supervisor, requesting that a new phone be added to your office area
   b. to another department head, suggesting a meeting to work out a problem between employees in your two areas
   c. to another division manager within your company, asking for increased support from the other division in meeting delivery schedules to your division

    d. to one of your employees, complimenting him or her on a job well done

2. Write a business letter on one of the following topics, creating fictitious company names, product lines, titles, and other information as needed:

    a. as a sales manager writing to a purchasing manager of another company, promoting one of your products

    b. as a prospective employee writing to an employer requesting consideration for a position

    c. as a director of a company's physical facilities writing to an electric utility company, requesting assistance with an energy audit of your company's facilities

    d. as a department manager writing to an office equipment company, requesting information and a sales presentation on a piece of office equipment, such as a typewriter, photocopier, or calculator

3. Prepare pages one and two of a report, as demonstrated in Figure 6.6. You may create fictitious information as needed to prepare such a report. Suggested topics:

    a. report of a meeting of department heads to discuss the company's plan

    b. report of a meeting of secretaries to plan a boss appreciation day

    c. results of a study done by your office on the need for a new company-wide newsletter for all employees

    d. results of a study analyzing use of a toll-free telephone number for taking customer orders

REFERENCES AND SUGGESTED READINGS

D'Aprix, Roger M. 1971. *How's That Again?* Homewood, Ill.: Dow Jones-Irwin.

Dawe, Jessamon, and Lord, William Jackson, Jr. 1974. *Functional Business Communication.* Englewood Cliffs, N.J.: Prentice-Hall.

Institute for Management. 1977. *The Dynamics of Business Communication.* Old Saybrook, Conn.: Institute for Management.

Lesikar, Raymond V. 1976. *Business Communication: Theory and Application,* 3rd ed. Homewood, Ill.: Richard D. Irwin.

Schneider, Arnold E., Donaghy, William C., and Newman, Pamela Jane. 1975. *Organizational Communication.* New York: McGraw-Hill.

Sigband, Norman B. 1976. *Communication for Management and Business.* Glenview, Ill.: Scott, Foresman.

Chapter 7

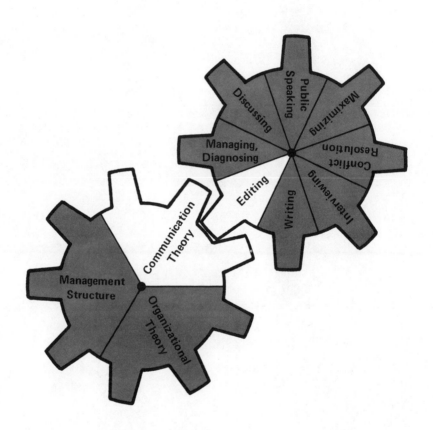

"Do This One Again"
SKILLS IN EDITING

This chapter will provide you with the following:

1. an appreciation for the need to edit business communications

2. the ability to identify the elements involved in a general editing review

3. an understanding of the components of a substantive editing review

4. the ability to identify and use the key components involved in a mechanical editing review

5. knowledge of and ability to use basic editing symbols

This chapter on editing follows the chapter on writing because, to be a good writer, you should also be a good editor. The purpose and function of an editor are very different from those of a writer, however, and good editing requires another set of skills.

Among the more important skills a writer should possess are creative ability and invention. A writer is encouraged to let thoughts flow—putting words down as they come to the mind without interruption in the creative process. An editor, however, uses more analytical skills. The editor's responsibility is to be critical of the words that are already written. This critical analysis requires stopping frequently to go back and review and review again. An editor, therefore, is not a creative writer but rather a critical reader. Even if you have produced the material you are editing, as an editor you must treat the written material with detachment—without concern for hurting the writer's feelings.

As an employee in a business organization, you certainly will be required to edit your own written material. For this process, you must set aside your creative abilities and learn to make a hard, critical review of your own innovative genius. In the business world, you may also be called upon to edit material for others, including supervisors. In such cases, you will have to take into consideration the person and personality of the writer while maintaining an analytical and critical approach to the material as much as possible. Make the tough editorial changes that are necessary, but avoid making changes in the aspects of the written words that reflect personal, stylistic choices based on the personality of the writer.

You may also have the opportunity to edit material that has been prepared by subordinates under your supervision. Use the editing time as a teaching and learning experience for your subordinates, helping them to improve their written style.

Cary S. Wolinsky/Stock, Boston, Inc.

Revising your work is not always pleasant but is almost always necessary

GENERAL EDITING REVIEW: THE OCAE SYSTEM

The OCAE (pronounced "okay") system[1] provides some guidelines to good writing that you should use in reviewing material to edit. These guidelines cover broad categories and represent areas that you should consider as part of your overall editing. Later in the chapter, we will discuss specific technical aspects of editing.

Organization

Regardless of the nature of the written material, organization is crucial if the written communication is to be successful. A pattern

[1] OCAE stands for organization, clarity, appropriateness, and emphasis.

is needed to assist the reader in following the thought process. The material you edit deserves several readings. The first reading should be general, giving attention to broad, nontechnical aspects. In this reading you should get a feeling for the organizational flow of the written document. You should look for four basic items:

1. In the introduction, make certain that things have been mentioned in the proper order—first things first—so that the piece clearly outlines its purpose.
2. In the body of the document, look for a specific order: topical, logical, chronological, spatial, or the like.
3. Make certain that there are transitions leading from point to point within the document.
4. Read the summary carefully to make sure that the most important points are restated.

Clarity

A businesslike, to-the-point approach is generally preferred for most writing used in the business world. This approach should not be confused with shortness or simplicity. Complex, detailed reports obviously are used in the business world, and they, too, should follow these principles of clarity. A thousand-page report with highly complex technical language can maintain clarity and be businesslike and to-the-point no matter how complex the technical detail is.

As you do your first general reading of the document to be edited, attempt to get a feeling for the clarity of the writing. On your second reading, when you start making technical corrections, your editing changes will be more consistent with the author's intent as a result of the first general reading. In editing for clarity, keep the following principles in mind:

1. The active voice is normally preferred over the passive voice.

    Active:　He bought the product from our competitor.

    Passive:　The product was bought from our competitor.

    Active:　That's why I fired him.

Passive: It is for that reason that he was fired.

In the active voice, the subject performs the action. In the passive voice, the subject is acted on.

2. Concrete words and phrases generally are much clearer than abstract words and phrases.

Concrete: The blue and green color contrast on that product is very appealing to me.

Abstract: I like that product.

Concrete: The $2,000 price is about $500 more than I had anticipated.

Abstract: That's just too expensive.

3. Words having fewer syllables usually are preferred over words having many syllables.

Fewer syllables: stubborn (two syllables)

Many syllables: cantankerous (four syllables)

Fewer syllables: great (one syllable)

Many syllables: fantastic (three syllables)

4. If a technical term must be used that might not be understood by readers, make sure that a straightforward explanation of the term is provided.

Unclarified technical term: Our analysis showed a historical trend projection of profit in 1990 at $5.5 million.

Explanation of technical term: Our analysis used the historical trend method of projection. A review of the past three years revealed profits of 1985, $1.5M; 1986, $2.1M; 1987, $2.8M. The historical trend method extends the historical pattern to a similar number of years in the future. Thus our 1985, 1986, and 1987 data can predict the following pattern: 1988, $3.6M; 1989, $4.5M; and 1990, $5.5M.

Appropriateness

It is difficult to prescribe appropriate language for business situations. Each writer and editor must necessarily make those judgmental decisions for the particular written document. As a general rule, however, business writers should avoid several potential pitfalls:

1. Avoid exaggeration. Terms such as *greatest, most outstanding, revolutionary, unbelievable,* and *sensational* should be avoided in order to maintain a higher level of believability by the readership.
2. Any indication of bitterness, anger, preaching, or other negativeness should be deleted, as these are generally considered inappropriate in business communications. (Figures 7.1 and 7.2 are examples of the negative style that should be avoided.)

Emphasis

Location is very important in business. The retail businessman knows that a business with excellent potential can be ruined by a poor geographical location. Industrial and corporate business leaders also understand the importance of location for access to transportation and labor markets, and for other reasons. Unfortunately, however, many people do not consider the importance of the physical location of points in a written communication and thus their relative emphasis. Keep the following points in mind when considering emphasis:

1. Position is important, especially what is stated first and what is stated last. The first portion of a written piece sets the tone and establishes a relationship between writer and reader. The last point mentioned tends to be remembered best. It is the writer's "parting shot," and it leaves a final impression with the reader.
2. The amount of space allocated to subjects is also important. Space allocation establishes a proportional relationship, so that more attention will be given to items that are given more space. Points that are given a large amount of space will often be perceived as more important. In editing a document, you should be aware of the amount of space

October 9, 1980
Mr. Monty Lovejoy
Chairman of the Board
First National Bank
Monsoon, Louisiana

Dear Mr. Lovejoy:

I am taking the time to inform you of my total disbelief in the decision
that has been made in recommending the AUTOmatic switch to your Board
of Directors.

Triple X and I are giving all we can in the way of support and service to
you and our customers in Monsoon. Two of the banks in your community
have chosen Triple X, but that means nothing because a company in Alex-
andria has the AUTOmatic switch. Triple X has 1,350 lines of telephones
installed in Monsoon, the other competitor has none to my knowledge.
Triple X is a 2 billion dollar company dedicated to service of our
customers, the competition is a one-man operation, which has little financial guarantee to you, the "end user." The Ace XXX is installed in 3,900 of
the largest companies in America; match customer lists. XYZ is the biggest
customer of Ace XXX.

Mr. Lovejoy, you and I have never had the opportunity to talk, so there is
no way for me to know what your understanding of telephone equipment
may be. Triple X and I want your business, and feel we deserve that
privilege.

I would also like to document this letter for our files for future reference.
There are quite a few companies in Monsoon interested in doing business
with Triple X and I don't want bad service or an inferior product to spoil
the name of interconnect companies in your community. We have worked
hard for our good name.

Sincerely,

TRIPLE X, INC.

Gary Gogetter
Marketing Representative

GG:na

FIGURE 7.1   Sample negative business letter

October 15, 1980

Chief Executive Officer
Triple X, Inc.
67890 Main Street
New York, New York

Dear Sir:

    I am enclosing a copy of a letter that we received from your
Marketing Representative. Needless to say, I am sure you can realize the
adverse reaction we will ever have toward dealing with your company in
the future after receiving a letter expressing such arrogance!

    We apologize for inconveniencing you by even giving your company
our consideration!!

                    Sincerely yours,

                    Monty Lovejoy
                    Chairman of the Board and
                    Chief Executive Officer
                    First National Bank

MJ:na

FIGURE 7.2   Sample negative business letter

    devoted to various points or issues and make sure that the
    ratio is appropriate.
3. Judicious use of underlining and exclamation points and
    similar methods of creating emphasis is vital. Overuse
    negates the value of these forms and renders them useless
    for emphasis.

TECHNICAL REVIEW

After a general reading of the document to be edited, the editor is
ready to deal with more technical issues. Technical editing con-

sists of two general categories: substantive review and mechanical review.

Substantive review

The substantive review should focus on three main areas: the opening, the basic content area of the communication, and the closing.

Opening Check the opening portion of the written communication carefully to make certain that the purpose of the communication is absolutely clear. The statement of purpose should come very early in the opening and should be easily identifiable. If the purpose is muddled by words or phrases that obscure it, as editor you will need to clarify the writing so that the statement of purpose is easily recognizable. The following examples of a first draft and its revision demonstrate this point:

SALESMAN'S FIRST DRAFT

Dear John:

The visit with you in your office the other day was most enjoyable. I especially liked the way you brought others into the discussion so that they could see how our system operates. We have found that users need to become very familiar with our system in order to overcome a basic fear to change from their current procedures to our modern technology. It may be that there are others in your organization who could also benefit from a demonstration. I think you may have said something about another department needing to see the demonstration. Was it the purchasing office or personnel? In any case, you know that we could work a presentation into our schedules if you think that it might be helpful.

EDITED REVISION

Dear John:

Thanks for a great visit with you last week. All of your people were so pleasant, eager to learn, and receptive. John, you indicated that perhaps your purchasing office employees might need a demonstration of our system. We are anxious to do this. Would next week be agreeable? Think about a good time for you and your people and I'll be back in touch by phone to arrange the details.

A quick statement of the purpose is especially important in business communications because business readers like to get directly to the heart of a matter. This is a businesslike expectation, and the editor should make sure that the communication clearly delivers its purpose.

Content area   A business reader seeks a pattern to the communication in the basic content area of the written communication. Often, signposts that enumerate points as first, second, third, and so forth, can be very helpful in demonstrating a pattern to the content area of the communication, regardless of the type of pattern used. The editor should examine the content area carefully to make certain that all portions are in a consistent order—logical, topical, sequential, chronological, spatial, or the like.

Closing   Business executives are fully aware of the significance of the closing in communication situations involving a sale. They know that the ability to obtain closure is crucial in a good sales representative. Thus, successful written communications in business need an excellent closing in order to be successful.

Normally, people remember best that which they hear last. For this reason, the closing portion of a business communication should reinforce the main point. As an editor, you should make certain that a forceful restatement of the main point occurs in the general closing area of a business communication.

Mechanical review

The mechanics of editing involve specific areas in the written piece where you may want to make changes. This is the time to get your editing pencil out and sharpen the point. It is a good idea to use a pencil that has an eraser, so that you can make changes, reflect on your changes, and possibly make additional changes. If you are working on a printed document that will be going to the printer, it is best to use a blue-lead pencil.

Paragraph length   Without considering the content or quality of the material, look at the document paragraph by paragraph to obtain a feeling for the paragraph lengths used. You should seek to keep paragraphs reasonably short and to have some consistency in paragraph length throughout the document. If you discover exceedingly long paragraphs, you should review them with an eye to breaking long paragraphs into two or three shorter paragraphs.

General uniformity in size of paragraphs gives a written document a very neat appearance, which can be important to the reader. While you are looking at paragraph lengths, it is a good time to check on the amount of space devoted to particular points. Remember that, generally, the greatest amount of space should be devoted to the most significant points in the document.

Word choice The selection of appropriate words and phrases is crucial to the success of a written communication. Word choice is also important in creating the recommended businesslike, to-the-point approach. The following are two examples of wordy and ambiguous statements that have been edited into a much more businesslike, to-the-point style:

FIRST DRAFT

I would like to point out for the record that I have attempted to make every opportunity available for Bob to succeed in his sales calls. Nevertheless, for a variety of reasons that I have not been able to isolate, Bob continues to demonstrate that he is having significant problems in meeting his sales quota.

EDITED REWRITE

I have done everything possible to help Bob succeed, but he continues to undersell his quota.

FIRST DRAFT

As you may know, our staff has been working for more than six months in an attempt to isolate the problem we have been experiencing with our general ledger. It now appears that it would be in our best interest to employ an outside consultant who could troubleshoot for us, isolate the problem, and assist us in rectifying this situation so that the program will function properly again.

EDITED REWRITE

After six months of unsuccessful effort by our staff in attempting to correct our general ledger program, I recommend we hire a consultant to help us solve the problem and get the program functioning properly again.

As you can see from these examples, word choice is important. It is easy in writing a first draft of a written document to get carried away with filler phrases. Writers frequently use many words that have ambiguous meanings, and the role of the editor is to sharpen the document by changing wordy phrases and eliminating unnecessary words. In the following list, the left column shows several wordy phrases and the right column provides a less wordy way to say the same thing:

Wordy	Less wordy
I would like to point out that	Since
You may be aware of the fact that	You probably know that
Due to the fact that	Since, because
Based on experience I can say	I have learned
Subsequent to	After

Repetition   Several types of repetition plague writers. The good editor will watch carefully for repetition and reduce or eliminate it. Some repetition may be useful, but the repeated use of a term, phrase, or slogan can quickly weaken its effectiveness. Normally, when a point needs to be made a second time, the editor should change the language so that the point is made through restatement rather than mere repetition. The following paragraph example demonstrates excessive repetition:

> Dear Sue:
>
> I appreciated your sending me your excellent report on our efficiency studies. The report was well done and was presented in a very attractive binder. Your good work in this report will be really helpful. I think the attractive folder will also be impressive. I just can't say enough about what a fine report it is and how attractively packaged it is. You have my sincere thanks for an excellent report attractively presented.
>
> Sincerely.
>
> Bob

The foregoing example may be exaggerated, but it shows how easily one can overstate a point through repetition. In the following example, the same sentiment is conveyed, but word choice has reduced repetition:

Dear Sue:

I appreciated your sending me your excellent report on our efficiency studies. I have carefully reviewed the document, and the high caliber of your work in this study will be a tremendous help to me! I was also impressed with the neat and functional folder used to transmit the report. Congratulations and thanks for a job well done.

Sincerely,

Bob

In larger documents, such as an extensive report or a long letter, the repetition or restatement may be spread throughout the report. The longer the written document you are working with, the more difficult it is to isolate repetition in the attempt to avoid it. If you begin to feel that you are coming across the same word, phrase, or expression repeatedly in a document, try noting their occurrence in pencil in the margin and then review to see if, in your judgment, the word or phrase has been used too frequently for it to carry a positive effect. If so, substitute another word or phrase or eliminate it.

Subject and verb agreement   Although a college graduate operating in the business world is assumed to have proper grammatical training, many grammatical problems will surface in business writing. One of the frequent problems—often a rather glaring mistake—is the agreement of subject and verb.

The following sentence has a plural subject with a singular verb:

These instruments was bought in 1980.

Here, *was* should be *were*, since the subject is plural. The same concept could be conveyed, however, in a sentence such as the following:

Every one of these instruments was bought in 1980.

In this case, *was* is the appropriate verb, since the subject, *one*, is singular.

Such confusion occurs with some frequency in writing, and the editor bears the responsibility of locating these problems in a review of the material. In most cases, a very quick editorial change will easily correct the situation and put the subject and verb in agreement.

Subject-verb-object format   In accordance with the businesslike, straightforward, to-the-point approach, business writing is generally more successful when sentences follow a standard format: subject first, verb next, and object last. This format is less subject to ambiguity and tends to be more direct and to the point. It seems to be a preferred style in business communication. The following sentence illustrates this format:

> The form for these documents should follow the prescribed order.

The first thing in this sentence is the subject, *form,* followed by the verb, *should follow,* which is followed by the object, *order.* Following is the same information conveyed in a different order; notice the awkwardness of the format:

> Concerning the form for these documents, the prescribed order should be followed.

Clarity   Word choice throughout a written document involves decisions concerning words and phrases that will express meaning clearly. Your judgment as editor may be substantially different from that of the person who wrote the document. You should keep personal preferences and personal style in mind as you change words or phrases to achieve greater clarity. If you feel you must make changes, be sure to consider the personality, choices, style, and characteristics of the individual named as principal author of the document.

  An editor should be alert to some specific areas in attempting to improve clarity. Two particular problem areas are frequently found in business correspondence. The first problem area is lack of identification. The editor should attempt to make certain that full identification is given when a person or product is first mentioned in a written document. In subsequent references to the person or product, an abbreviated reference can be made, unless the subsequent references are infrequent and widely separated from the original reference by large amounts of written material, in which case the full identification should be repeated.

In the following example, the letter does not fully identify Charles Moore, who is referred to in the letter:

> Dear John:
>
> I received your letter asking for clarification of several points on our bid specifications. I am asking Charles Moore to come by to see you in a few days to clarify these points. I think that this opportunity to discuss this personally will be best for both of us.
>
> Thanks for the opportunity to be of service to you.
>
> Sincerely,
>
> Jim

Unless John just happens to know Charles Moore, he will not know Charles Moore's position and will not be able to reach him if he needs to contact him before the meeting. The following is a revised version of the letter:

> Dear John:
>
> I received your letter asking for clarification of several points on our bid specifications. I am asking Charles Moore, our engineer who developed the specifications, to come by to see you in a few days to clarify these points. I think that this opportunity to discuss this personally will be best for both of us.
>
> Thanks for the opportunity to be of service to you.
>
> Sincerely,
>
> Jim

In this instance, the inclusion of the descriptive information, "our engineer who developed the specifications," gives John a much better idea about the person Charles Moore. Additional clarification could be given later in the letter, with the addition of a telephone number where Charles Moore could be reached.

Another problem area is the use of technical terms. When you are working with a particular set of technical terms very frequently, you may fall into the habit of using the terms without thinking that explanation might be needed. You and the people you work with may know and understand the terms, but you should define them if you think they might be unfamiliar to the reader.

Basic symbols of editing   The following is a list of the key symbols used in editing. These symbols are standard and generally accepted, and your use of them will clearly identify your intent to others who may be reviewing your work. This is not a comprehensive list, but it represents the most frequently used and most commonly understood symbols, which should suffice unless you are extensively involved in editing:

Symbol	Meaning
¶	New paragraph
⌒	Exchange location
∧	Insert
ℓ	Delete
≡	Capitalize
——	Italicize

¶ Now is the time for all good men to come to aid of their country—the united states.

Spelling   Keep a dictionary or spelling dictionary nearby. A writer might not stop the thought flow to confirm a particular spelling, but the editor certainly must catch misspellings. No business organization wants to be represented by the sloppy work that poor spelling indicates.

Neatness   Looks can be deceiving! A beautifully represented document with weak content will often win out over a sloppy document with excellent content. Your organization wants the best of both worlds—excellent content, attractively packaged. Such a combination offers the best assurance of success.

SUMMARY

This chapter discussed the role of editing in reviewing business communications. The basic principles of the OCAE system—organization, clarity, appropriateness, and emphasis—were covered, with specific guidelines for each of these aspects. Editing also requires a technical review of the substantive material, including the opening, content, and closing of business communications. Examination of the technical and mechanical review included paragraph length, word choice, repetition, subject and verb agreement, the subject-verb-object format, clarity, editing symbols, spelling, and neatness.

EXERCISES

1. Write a critique of the business letters in Figures 7.1 and 7.2. In your critique, demonstrate your ability to perform a substantive editing review.
2. Using the business letters in Figures 7.1 and 7.2, demonstrate your ability to perform a mechanical editing review.
3. Copy the following sample and then review it, showing your ability to perform substantive and mechanical editing.

Dear Mary,

I certainly would like to express my sincere appreciation to you and to all of those in your office area who in any way had a part in hosting me during my visit with your firm last week. I think that I can truthfully say that I have seldom been treated in a more royal fashion in all my years of business than I was treated by you and all of your associates in my visit with you last week.

What I would like to convey to you is that I have a sincere interest in trying to service your firm by meeting your production needs. It is my considered opinion that you would find our well-trained professional staff contains all of the areas of expertise which your firm would likely need, and we could assure you, therefore, that you should probably be most satisfied as clients of our firm.

Mary, if there is any question whatsoever which you have or might have in the future, please don't hesitate a minute to just pick up the phone and call me or to write me a letter explaining the question you might have. We promise you that we will respond in the quickest timeframe possible and as completely as possible to assure you total and complete satisfaction.

We are certainly looking forward with great anticipation to a long and profitable association with your firm.

Sincerely,

4. Copy the following sample exactly, and then perform a mechanical edit, showing your ability to use editing symbols.

Dear Roger,

I wanted to let you know the exact time of my arrival on Trans world airways flight #123 which will arrivethe Airport at 11.20 A.M. I'll be looking forward too seeing you. By the way, if you have a chance it would be nice if you could bring Mary ann with you. We are old friends from High School days and I would really like to see her. I was delighted to learn that she was working with you now. Again, I'll be looking forward to seeing you at the Airport.

Sincerely,

REFERENCES AND SUGGESTED READINGS

Turabian, Kate L. 1973. *A Manual for Writers of Term Papers, Theses, and Dissertations,* 4th ed. Chicago: University of Chicago Press.
Uris, Auren. 1975. *Memos for Managers.* New York: Thomas L. Crowell. Sec. 10.
Weiss, Allen. 1977. *Write What You Mean.* New York: AMACOM. Ch. 12.

Chapter 8

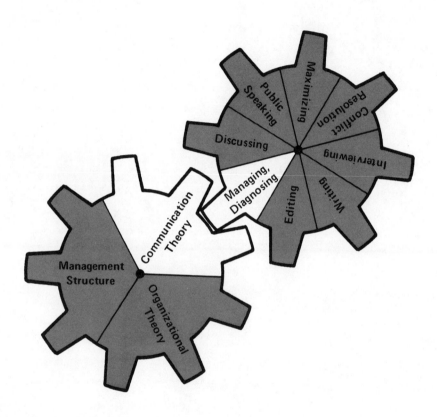

"I Thought You Understood"

SKILLS IN DIAGNOSING AND MANAGING COMMUNICATION PROBLEMS

This chapter will provide you with the following:

1. an awareness of typical business communication problems

2. the ability to identify communication problems

3. the ability to identify and use strategies for tracing problems

4. the ability to identify and use techniques for managing communications

This chapter deals with the variety of misunderstandings that may develop quickly in small and large business organizations. Considerable material has been published elsewhere detailing communication problems in business and industry. Although the material in this chapter is not designed to be exhaustive, it does indicate many of the potential problem areas in communication.

The problem areas considered here are information overload, dissemination breakdown, bottlenecks, rumor chain, and grapevine, and an assortment of other barriers to communication. Lest you think that there are only problems with communication, we will also provide a review of strategies and techniques for tracing problems, as well as a set of recommendations for creating good communication and for managing communication effectively.

COMMUNICATION PROBLEMS

There are many ways to describe and categorize the variety of problems encountered in business communication. Our efforts in this section have focused on several categories that typify the more common or frequent problem areas.

Information overload

Although some writers indicate that there is a need for excessive communication (D'Aprix, 1971), it is generally believed that too much information can create serious communication problems in an organization. Because of the diversity of the constituencies within an organization, it is necessary to repeat messages through various channels and in different ways to make certain that the message is communicated appropriately to all individuals who need to receive the information. This process is not considered information overload; rather, it is an appropriate repetition of information. Information overload occurs when specific information for a specific person or group of people is targeted toward that individual or group of people excessively, resulting in rejection of some or all of the information.

Information overload may occur in several forms. One such form is "memoitis." This involves the overuse of memoranda to repeat instructions or otherwise communicate. Some people tend to use memoranda as their primary means of communication. As described elsewhere in this book, memoranda can be very effec-

"I thought you understood..."

Burt Glinn/Magnum Photos, Inc.

tive communication tools, but their overuse is also possible. Repeated use of memos to reinforce a single topic can cause the recipients of the memos to reject the communication because of a feeling of harassment.

Overuse of memoranda can also involve using the memorandum format too frequently, though on a variety of topics. The manager who relies heavily on the use of memoranda for communicating his or her desires for subordinates' action on a large number of issues can destroy the effectiveness of the memo form. When the subordinates receive so many memoranda dealing with relatively small and insignificant items that the sheer mass of memos creates overloads on their minds, they may completely reject dealing with the memos. They may hope that the memo sender will forget about the memos and that there will be no negative repercussions from failure to follow through with the requests. This overload might be called the "Oh, no! Another memo!" syndrome.

Information overload can also occur in organizations through documentation in manuals. In our highly mechanized, computerized society, careful documentation of computer programs and operating procedures for highly specialized equipment is crucially important. Massive documentation can create information overload, however, causing the person working with the documentation to reject the written manuals because of sheer size. This tendency can be lessened by the use of excellent tables of contents or indexes to assist a person working with very large documentation manuals. Training programs on how to work with the manuals can also be helpful. If an employee is just handed a massive operating manual and told "That's got all the info you need," overload may result.

Sometimes managers may ask several subordinates to review the same problem, planning to compare the various reports. A meeting may be called with the subordinates to discuss their varying perspectives or possible solutions to the problem. The danger in using such a procedure is that the subordinates may feel that an inordinate amount of time and effort has been put into a project that someone else was doing, and they may feel their time has been wasted. They may develop the attitude that, if someone else is going to be working on the same project, they should not commit their time to it. The manager, in addition to suffering from possible hard feelings among the subordinates, may learn more about the problem than was desired. Thus, a manager can be victimized by obtaining too much information from subordinates: "Now that I've got all this info, what do I do?"

A person can also experience information overload by receiving essentially the same information from a variety of sources. An employee might attend a staff meeting at which certain information is disseminated. Later, the employee might receive a written report dealing with the same subject. Still later, the person might receive a memorandum from a supervisor, together with a carbon copy of several letters that deal with the same subject. In such cases, the employee may begin to suffer from information overload.

A severe problem with information overload is its tendency to create in the recipient a "turn off" attitude. The recipient of the repetitive information or overload develops negative feelings, shuts out all future information on that topic, and perhaps even selectively forgets already received information. The automatic shut-out of additional information could cause serious problems for that employee, because future communication on the same subject, though containing some repetitious information, might also contain some additional information that is vitally needed.

Dissemination breakdowns

Most organizations frequently need to communicate information within the organization and are occasionally engaged in careful planning to disseminate information outside the organization. This need to communicate requires an organization-wide plan to provide a comprehensive strategy for success. Although most businesses would not think of developing a new product that would need to be marketed without a carefully devised marketing strategy, unfortunately many organizations and businesses do not exercise the same thoroughness in planning an overall communication strategy for internal or external communication. Employee communication within an organization often suffers from a lack of careful planning on the part of upper management.

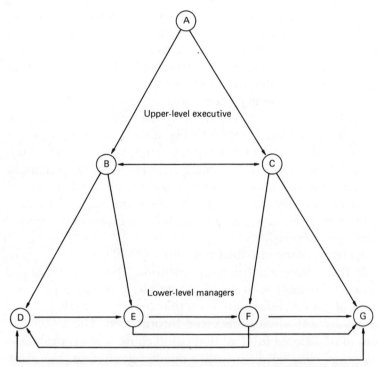

A can communicate with D-G only by going through B-C, who act as filters. D and E get information from B, while F and G get information from C. Since B and C may have shared A information to subordinates in slightly different ways, D and E may have different information from F and G. Since D and E can talk horizontally with F and G, however, they will become aware that they have received different messages. Confusion, uncertainty, and mistakes can result.

FIGURE 8.1   Downward and horizontal information chains

Many organizations rely on informal communication networks, which may or may not work in any given case. An informal process will probably occur in some form, yet it cannot be relied on for consistent communication effectiveness. Some organizations rely on supervisors to disseminate information to subordinates as a method of downward communication. Again, because of the personal nature of the communication, such a networking system allows too much opportunity for miscommunication (see Figure 8.1).

Since organizations need a method for communicating information throughout the organization, a written form of communication, such as a newsletter, is necessary. This provides a formal record of what was communicated and assures precision of communication, with much more accuracy than would occur with the oral method of supervisors communicating to subordinates. An oral communication network of information-sharing meetings should be a supplement to a newsletter type of publication.

Bottlenecks

A communication bottleneck can occur in several different ways. A company newsletter that is distributed to only part of the management team of the organization will be a bottleneck in itself, because the information will not be disseminated throughout the organization. Another frequent bottleneck in organizations is the employee who is either lazy or not well organized and does not fulfill a communication responsibility to share information with others. Thus, a bottleneck in communication occurs when an organization plans or intends for a person or a procedure to disseminate information adequately, but some portion of the communication system—either an individual or a communication organism—fails to fulfill its responsibility.

Rumor chain and grapevine

There is much popular discussion about the significance of the grapevine and rumor chain as important communication channels in organizations. Figures 8.2 and 8.3 show how these channels work. Although these forms of communication channels exist to varying degrees in many organizations, their effect can be positive or negative, depending on the understanding and use made of them by individuals within the organization. Essentially, rumor is created information. It is information created by a disinterested third party—a secondary source rather than a primary source. The same is true of information on the grapevine. The so-called creation of information through rumor or grapevine normally oc-

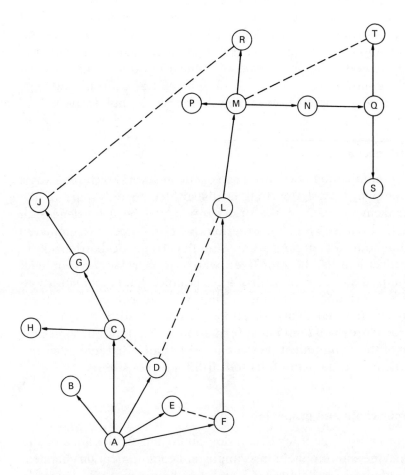

———————— Direct contact by one individual to another. A, for example, communicates
with selected individuals, some of whom communicate the information to
others.

— — — — Potential contacts (secondary/reinforcement sources) make it possible for a
person to get the information from more than one source.

FIGURE 8.2   Grapevine chain

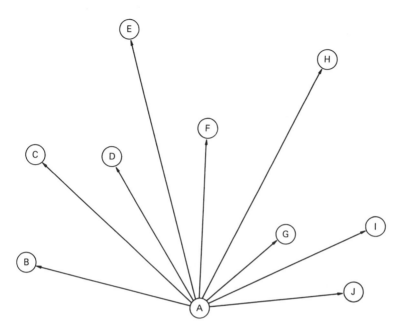

A tells information to as many people as A desires. Each recipient of A may set off
entirely new rumor chains.

FIGURE 8.3   Rumor chain

curs because there is a lack of information coming from a primary
source. One way organizations can deal with this problem is to
make sure that adequate information comes from the primary
source—that is, the organization itself—through a newsletter or
other communication vehicle.

Rumor can also result from a lack of trust among individuals.
If people have determined through previous experiences that they
cannot trust the communication disseminated by others, mistrust
sets in. In some people, this mistrust may lead to the creation of information in keeping with their perceptions of a situation.

The best way for a company to deal with the grapevine and
rumor chain is to have a plan for effective communication and to
deal openly, honestly, and forthrightly with employees. The
organization's communication mouthpiece, in whatever form, can
help keep positive communication with "the company line" di-

rected to employees. The existing grapevines or chains can also be used by an organization, by finding the informal chains and links and infiltrating them with the information the company wants passed on.

Davis (1953) expressed a rather commonly held viewpoint about grapevines: "No administrator in his right mind would ever try to abolish the management grapevine. . . . It should be recognized, analyzed, and consciously used for better communication."

Other barriers to communication

1. *Distance.* The physical placement of offices sometimes creates problems in maintaining effective communication among employees. Employees who need to communicate most closely should be located in close proximity to one another if at all possible.
2. *Inaccessibility.* Individuals who need to communicate with others should have clear opportunities for communication without bureaucratic barriers or other delaying devices. Supervisors must keep open lines of accessibility for subordinates.
3. *Distortion.* This occurs when a person is receiving mixed signals. Several individuals within an organization might be communicating different information to the same individual, and the inconsistency of the various communications might result in distorted communication.
4. *Incompatibility.* Occasionally, if two or more individuals seem to be personally incompatible, this will affect their ability to communicate effectively.
5. *Lack of trust.* Trust is crucial to effective communication. If people do not have a sense of trust, it is difficult for them to communicate well.
6. *Balance or leveling.* Communication within organizations can come from various levels. If those at the executive level, for example, use too much force or are perceived as using too much force by a subordinate employee, an order or

directive from upper level management can become a communication barrier. Some employees will react to a perceived overuse of force with stubbornness and outright rejection.

STRATEGIES AND TECHNIQUES FOR TRACING PROBLEMS: THE COMMUNICATION AUDIT

No business or organization would consider operating for a year without a comprehensive financial audit. Few business organizations, however, engage regularly in a communication audit. The parallel is an accurate one, because the communication audit, which has only recently come into prominence, performs for the communication side of an organization precisely what a financial audit performs for the business side of the organization. The communication audit is designed to identify for an organization what communications are occurring, when they are occurring, where they are occurring, and who is involved in the communications. An audit trail allows a trained person to trace communication problems to the source.

The process of a comprehensive communication audit is extremely complex and will not be discussed in detail in this chapter, but we will briefly describe several of the key elements of a communication audit, which can be helpful to a student of business communication.

We are particularly concerned with tracing problems that might be perceived within an organization. Since the audit attempts to describe what is and has been occurring, it can plot communication experiences in a format that will allow some tracing.

Telephone log

A telephone log is part of the communication audit. The purpose of the telephone log is to secure information about telephone calls occurring throughout an organization. This normally must be done on an individual basis, following the format shown in Figure

8.4. The log records the time of a telephone conversation, the people involved, and the subject matter. With this information, an individual can plot telephone habits of employees. If there has been a communication problem between certain employees, the telephone log might assist in tracing the problem or identifying some of its characteristics.

Correspondence log

A correspondence log is designed to obtain factual information about correspondence that passes through an office. It can be maintained on a unit or office-wide basis or individually. The purpose of the correspondence log is to record information about each piece of correspondence that comes into the office and each piece of correspondence that leaves the office. Samples of correspondence logs are given in Figures 8.5 and 8.6.

As you can see in the samples, the information recorded on such logs will identify who is writing whom, how many times within a given period correspondence is occurring between individuals, the nature of the correspondence, and other reference points. One of the finer points that can be determined from a correspondence log is the type of action being taken on written requests. The log indicates when a written request has been made and demonstrates who should act on it and within what timeframe the action should occur. Additional tracing through the correspondence log will indicate whether or not the request was met on a timely basis.

Personal time log

For employees whose contacts are more personal, a personal time log may be used. This log records a person's actions at short time intervals throughout the day. This log is only used periodically, since it is extremely time consuming. Occasional use of such a log can be helpful, however, in tracing the communication patterns of employees.

TELEPHONE LOG

Date

Employee Name

Time Initiated	Time Concluded	Other Party	Request Information	Give Information	Request Action	Give Action	Request Follow-up	Requires Transfer to Another Party	Other

Check as Appropriate

FIGURE 8.4 Telephone log

CORRESPONDENCE LOG
Incoming

Date | Office

To	Subject	Disposition	Date of Disposition

FIGURE 8.5   Incoming correspondence log

CORRESPONDENCE LOG
Outgoing

Date		Office	

To	Subject	Disposition	Date of Disposition

FIGURE 8.6   Outgoing correspondence log

Corporate records

A full communication audit would also look at all corporate communication vehicles. Internal newsletters would be examined, and external communication pieces would be reviewed. Bulletin boards and printed announcement areas would be monitored. These and other methods of obtaining and recording information about communication within organizations can be very helpful. We have included here those checks that you can use most effectively on a personal basis.

STRATEGIES AND TECHNIQUES FOR GOOD COMMUNICATION MANAGEMENT

First and foremost for good communication management, an organization needs a comprehensive plan. This communication plan should identify all the various constituent groups, both internal and external to the organization, with whom communication must be maintained regularly or periodically. For each constituent group, there should be an indication of the type of organizational communication in which it is engaged. Then a method or means should be determined by which that communication will occur. This comprehensive plan will assure as much as possible that important and effective communication is being maintained in all vital areas with all important constituent groups.

An organization should plan to conduct a comprehensive communication audit annually. In addition, spot audits should be taken from time to time, especially when trouble occurs. The use of spot audits will alert employees to the fact that their communication habits are being monitored occasionally, and this should make them more sensitive to good communication habits.

The use of a correspondence log can help improve organizational communication. The correspondence log should indicate that there has been timely response, providing information as requested. This is an important characteristic of effective communication.

Formal and informal methods and vehicles for communicating within the organization should be planned. Each employee should consider the other employees with whom he or she needs to communicate. A plan for regular and irregular, formal and informal contacts with these individuals will assure good and productive communication.

SUMMARY

Several of the more common communication problems encountered in business were described under the headings of information overload, dissemination breakdown, bottlenecks, and rumor chain and grapevine. Other barriers to communication were identified as distance, inaccessibility, distortion, incompatibility, lack of trust, and balance or leveling.

Discussion of strategies and techniques for tracing communication problems within an organization focused on the value of the communication audit. This procedure was described and sample worksheets were provided to help in implementing an audit. A telephone log, correspondence log, and personal time use log were discussed as part of the process on tracing communication problems through an organization to uncover areas where they may exist.

The need for a well-planned, comprehensive communication program for the organization was stressed. The program should assure that appropriate information is disseminated both within and outside the organization.

EXERCISES

1. Ask two friends to assist you in a communication experiment. Arrange to miss a portion of a campus meeting or class that you would normally attend. Have a friend attend the meeting or class to take careful notes for you. Arrange for another friend to tape-record the meeting or class that you miss. Listen to the recording and compare what actually transpired with the material in the notes. Write a paper identifying the differences you find between the written notes and the tape recording. Try to identify specific communication problems that might have caused the differences.

2. Have members of the class participate in a communication chain. Have all members of the class but one leave the room and wait in the hallway or in an adjacent room. Give the remaining student a statement of information to relate to another student. The statement should contain some factual information and a reasonable amount of detail, such as:

   a. "I saw a Corvette crash into a Dodge van the other day at the corner of West 51st Street and South Beard Avenue. Police and ambulance crews were on the scene, but I'm not sure if anyone was seriously hurt."

   b. "Three or four of us went out to a fraternity party after the game with a couple of the yell leaders. About halfway through the party we decided to go to my friend's apartment to start our own party. One of the yell leaders got sick and had to leave early, so the rest of us decided to go back to the fraternity party. It got so happy there that we decided just to call it a night."

   After giving the first student the story, have each student in the waiting area come into the classroom, one at a time, until all have participated. As each student enters the room, have the student who just heard the story repeat it. Continue the process until the story has been repeated individually to each student and by each student. Have the last student to enter the room repeat the story by writing it for the entire class to see. Compare the story as repeated by the last student with the original story you gave the first student. The instructor or one or two students should observe the entire series of story repetitions and attempt to identify the significant points at which the story changes. Discuss this process in class as an example of what happens in a communication chain.

3. Using an organization or class in which you are involved, or a work experience if you are currently employed, isolate an example of information overload, dissemination breakdown, or rumor or grapevine communication in action. Write a paper describing the circumstances surrounding the communication phenomenon, how it happened, results, and any other perspectives you have on the problem.

4. After reading the following case study, what actions would you take in this situation if you were John Lamb? Write a brief essay explaining your rationale for the actions you propose.

Case study: Alpha-Omega Company

Alpha-Omega Company produces cosmetics and home goods products that are sold by independent home-marketing dealers throughout the country. Over the past five years, sales have mushroomed and profits have increased at an equally amazing rate.

Sue Sholts has supervised the sales records office for the past three years. She is a true believer in the company and is deeply committed to her work. She has watched her division grow quickly, and she has put together a staff of employees to handle the workload. She is very proud of the organization that she has developed and is very supportive of the people she has employed. Sue frequently reminds the employees that they are working for a superstar company and that their personal financial success is assured by the rapid growth of the company. Sue's favorite line to her staff is, "Keep up the good work and do what they tell you to do and you can't help but be promoted."

Recently, the company offered Sue a chance for a promotion—as a regional sales liaison. It was a lucrative offer, and Sue jumped at the chance. John Lamb was transferred from another department to take Sue's former job. John came from the accounting department, where he had established himself as a very competent and tough-minded assistant. The staff in the sales records office hated to see Sue leave, especially because they had heard a lot of rumors that John was a really tough administrator.

Soon after John took over in the sales records office, he began to hear of rumblings among his new staff. He also was analyzing his new office staff and structure, and it seemed clear to him that the department was overstaffed. He heard by way of the grapevine that several employees had been promised raises by Sue, but in John's opinion these employees were in no way suitable for promotion, and he thought pay raises for them were unreal. Soon the staff in the sales records office began to hear rumors about John's evaluation of their office and some of his plans for cutbacks.

REFERENCES AND SUGGESTED READINGS

D'Aprix, Roger M. 1971. *How's That Again?* Homewood, Ill.: Dow Jones-Irwin.

Davis, Keith. 1953. "Management Communication and the Grapevine." *Harvard Business Review* 31: 43–49.

Kell, Carl L., and Corts, Paul R. 1980. *Fundamentals of Effective Group Communication.* New York: Macmillan.

Kirkpatrick, Donald L. 1978. *No-Nonsense Communication.* Brookfield, Wis.: K & M Publications.

Lesikar, Raymond V. 1976. *Business Communications: Theory and Application*, 3rd ed. Homewood, Ill.: Richard D. Irwin. Pp. 72–90.

Chapter 9

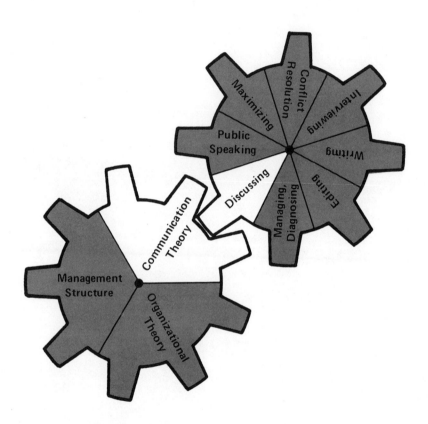

"Let's Discuss This"

SKILLS IN GROUP DISCUSSION FOR CONFERENCES AND MEETINGS

This chapter will provide you with the following:

1. an appreciation for the extensive role of group discussion in business organizations
2. an understanding of when to use groups most effectively
3. an understanding of the reasons for holding conferences, meetings, and group discussions
4. the ability to prepare for a meeting effectively
5. the ability to conduct a meeting effectively through task and social dimension processes
6. the ability to evaluate the effectiveness of a meeting

Professional leaders in business, industry, government, and other organizations spend a substantial amount of time in group discussion with other people. In the world of business, "according to various studies, managers spend up to fifty percent of their time in meetings" (Golde, 1972). Some people find it frustrating to have to spend so much time in meetings; however, the use of groups in contemporary business and industry is very valuable. Group discussion seems to be increasing as part of the decision-making process in business.

Group discussion is defined as three or more individuals interacting cooperatively through purposeful communication. There are three essential elements to this definition. First, individuals must give up some personal identity in permitting themselves to unite with other individuals to create a group. Second, the process of group discussion requires that individuals interact with one another in a cooperative spirit. Third, group discussion requires directed communication among the participants—that is, communication with a definite purpose.

It is important to remember the three elements of this definition. There will be times when groups of three or more individuals get together and interact orally with one another but group discussion is not necessarily occurring. During a coffee break, for example, a group of employees may sit around the employee lounge enjoying coffee and chatting. Such a gathering would meet some, but not all, of the criteria for group discussion as defined here. In business there are many times however, when formal group discussion does occur, and you might be asked to be a participant in the process. This chapter is designed to help prepare you for those occasions.

USES OF GROUP DISCUSSION

If you reflect on your activities and uses of time over the past few days or weeks, you will discover that you have spent a significant amount of time in group discussion. Many of these activities oc-

Small group communication skills often dominate a business environment

curred informally and were not structured. You will probably realize, however, that you have participated in a number of structured discussions. Group discussion occurs in our homes, in social clubs, in organizations, at churches, and in our government system.

Many large businesses and corporations have instituted executive leadership groups to make key decisions for their organizations. This contemporary practice contrasts with the former style of individual leadership. The days of barons, tycoons, or industrial giants singlehandedly domineering a corporation or business entity are mostly past. Contemporary practice relies on group thinking and group decision making from the highest levels of management down through the organization.

Most major policy decisions for an organization are made in board meetings, at which directors or key executives of corporations review facts, make judgments, and make collective decisions. Thus, the process of group discussion is at work in setting corporate or organizational policy.

Within an industrial organization, a group of engineers and designers might work jointly on product design and development. The expertise, skills, and perspectives of several individuals will be brought together in a group format so that the corporation can obtain the best possible advice on the design and development of new products.

Similarly, an organization will rely on a group of people to make sales and marketing decisions, using a variety of individuals with particular knowledge about specific segments of the market. A collective decision is considered superior to a decision made by a single individual, whose perspective is more limited than the collective view of a group of individuals. Thus, a group will be used to chart a marketing plan and sales program collectively.

Not only will you find a number of opportunities for the use of group discussion within your profession, you will also find that society at large uses the group discussion method. Our government system, which honors government of the people and by the people, requires that we use the group discussion process. Our individual points of view are voiced through the deliberative bodies of our government, such as the Congress, the state legislature, and the city council. These deliberative bodies also use group discussion to arrive at collective decisions. Thus, the very foundation of our American system of government promotes and encourages participation through group discussion.

Our social and community life is also centered on group processes that encourage group discussion. Such organizations as the Parent-Teacher Association, political parties, the YMCA/YWCA, churches, synagogues, and others, rely heavily on group discussion. These organizations may have large meetings that are run according to parliamentary procedure, but they often also have many small groups that meet to interact and discuss matters. Participation of individual members is what helps our organizations function, and most of us will be members of many organizations, formal and informal, that in some way will use group discussions.

THE PROCESS OF GROUP DISCUSSION

Group discussion is not static, and it does not occur in a vacuum. It can be characterized as a process that flows in the stream of time. The purpose for a group discussion will have evolved from some need, and at the conclusion of the group discussion there undoubtedly will be a need for action to take place as a result of the discussion. There is a sequential pattern of development within group discussion, as discussed by Tubbs (1978). Tubbs conceptualized small group interaction in the format of a systems approach. Our discussion in this text will attempt to isolate the component parts of the system and describe the process.

The simple five-step communication model in Figure 9.1 may help you see the process that occurs in normal communication. This model demonstrates that communication follows a predictable pattern from a source, which initiates a message to communicate, through an encoder, which puts the message into some form for transmission. The message then proceeds through a

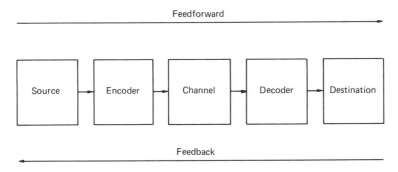

FIGURE 9.1　Simple communication model

channel. As the message comes through the channel, it is received by a decoder, which takes the message, interprets it, and passes it on to the final destination.

In normal communication, the general movement of the process, which is forward from the source to the destination, is called feedforward. A similar process occurs in the receipt of information, however, and the destination element of the process may also communicate back to the source. The reverse of the forward movement of the process is known as feedback. With this model, therefore, you can sense the movement that occurs in the communication process.

The model demonstrates the system of communication and the sequential pattern that follows naturally from that system. A similar process occurs in group discussion. Since a group is involved, however, the process becomes more complicated, because there are series of communication links between the multiple participants in a group discussion. Notice, also, that this process must occur for communication to be successful. The source cannot jump to the destination without proceeding through the intervening steps in the process.

Research in the field of group discussion has identified many different ways in which groups develop and many processes through which group action occurs. Gulley and Leathers (1977) present an excellent review of the literature on this subject. As an introduction to the subject we have chosen to deal with two dimensions that relate to group discussion—the task and the social dimension processes—and to describe the subcategories of these processes. We believe that this will help you to understand the most crucial elements of the group discussion process without burdening you with excessive detail. An elaboration of these processes will be given later in the chapter.

FORMAT FOR GROUP DISCUSSION

There are two basic formats in which group discussion occurs. One format, referred to as open or public, is depicted in Figure 9.2. An open or public format assumes that there is an audience watching the group discussion and participating in the actual discussion. The second format, closed or private, is illustrated in Figure

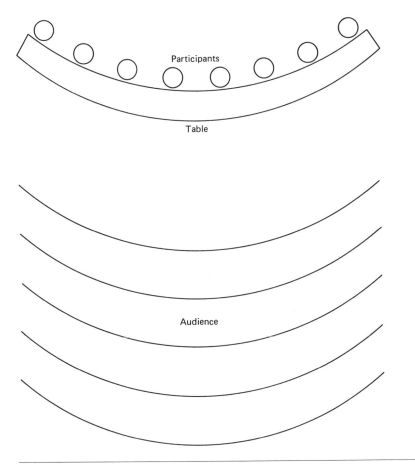

FIGURE 9.2   Open or public group arrangement

9.3. The closed or private discussion format assumes that only those people actively participating in the group are a part of the discussion process, and there is no audience.

Most meetings and conferences that occur in business organizations use the closed or private format. Generally, this format has several advantages. People feel less restrained in speaking because there is no uninvolved audience observing them; therefore, they tend to be more candid in sharing their personal opinions and beliefs with other participants. In addition, with this format group members are not distracted by the public audience and

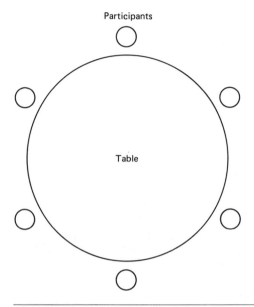

FIGURE 9.3   Closed or private group arrangement

therefore tend to give more singular attention to the matters under discussion. Finally, closed groups tend to develop greater solidarity among group participants.

STRENGTHS OF GROUP DISCUSSION

"Two heads are better than one." "United we stand, divided we fall." "The more the merrier." Such quotations represent the popular feeling in our contemporary society; we value small group communication. The value may be in increased knowledge, in increased resources, or in increased merriment, but in all cases there seems to be a feeling that there is increased value in a group.

We should acknowledge here that some researchers have pointed out many weaknesses in the communication process of group discussion. Several authors, including Smith (1965) and Cartwright and Zander (1968) deal with the weaknesses or limitations of small group communication as well as some of its strengths. In this chapter, however, we are interested in dealing with the strengths of group discussion.

Group thought power

There can be increased thought power through use of a group. Each of us is limited in our ability to provide information or make a judgment about any given topic. No matter how bright an individual may be, there is a limit to the capacity he or she has to possess information or to view a perspective or to generate ideas. Thus, great benefit is to be obtained from the pooling of resources in the small group. The multiplication of information held by individual members is a significant advantage to the group. The potential for a new perspective is substantially enhanced and the potential for generating new ideas on a subject is considerably expanded through the group process.

Figure 9.4 is a pictorial representation of increased thought power through a group arrangement. In the figure, of six indi-

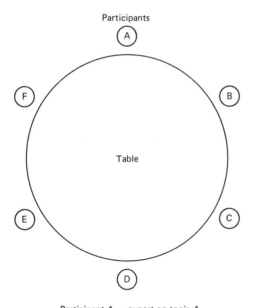

Participant A — expert on topic A
Participant B — expert on topic B
Participant C — expert on topic C
Participant D — good general overview
Participant E — good general overview
Participant F — good general overview

FIGURE 9.4   Group thought power

viduals participating in a group discussion, three possess special expertise on one phase of the total topic. The three other members of the group were invited to participate in the discussion because it was felt that they had a good general knowledge of the topic. The collection of the resources of these six individuals into a group will produce considerably greater potential than could have been attained from any one individual. The potential for thorough viewing of the problem from a variety of perspectives has been increased markedly.

Group manpower

Group discussion can provide additional manpower and thus can provide additional resources for accomplishing tasks. When groups have specific tasks that need to be accomplished, they often find it useful to subdivide responsibilities for accomplishing those tasks. The purpose for this subdivision might be to separate investigation of the matter, determination of possible solutions, and other exploration of the issue. In a group of six discussion participants, two may be assigned to take on one subresponsibility, two to take on another subresponsibility, and two others to take on a third specific subresponsibility. In this way, the six individuals can subdivide the work to lessen the burden on each individual within the group and to increase the productivity of the group as a whole. After all participants have done their individual work, they can meet as a group and share results. Figure 9.5 illustrates such an arrangement. Through this procedure, the whole group benefits from the information obtained through the subdivided process, yet each member did not have to go out and perform each of the tasks.

Group commitment

Group discussion helps in developing acceptance by those who participate in the process. Involving people in the information dissemination or problem-solving process gives them a better appreciation for the problem. If several individuals are involved in

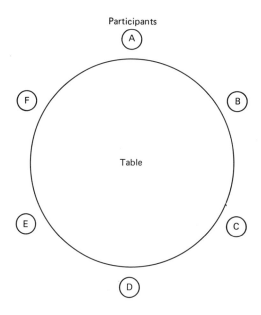

Participant A — researches topic A
Participant B — researches topic A
Participant C — conducts a survey with D
Participant D — conducts a survey with C
Participant E — researches topic B and conducts personal interviews with F
Participant F — researches topic B and conducts personal interviews with E

FIGURE 9.5 Group manpower

developing the solution through the group discussion process, they become committed to the solution.

Figure 9.6 depicts a possible group arrangement. In the figure, six individuals have formed a group to discuss a problem and develop a solution. After carefully reviewing the problem and analyzing possible solutions, the group eventually worked out a solution that was the result of participation by all members. Although each participant may have had an independent position initially, after they all presented their individual viewpoints, the group process molded the individual positions into one group position. After being part of this process, each discussion participant is committed to the final solution, because a portion of his or

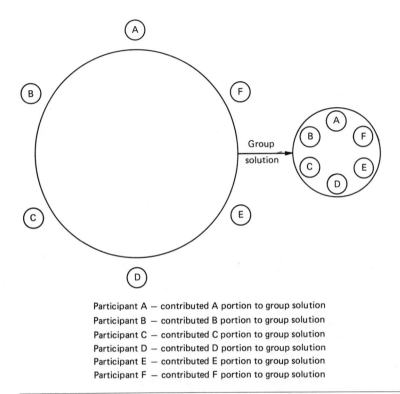

Participant A — contributed A portion to group solution
Participant B — contributed B portion to group solution
Participant C — contributed C portion to group solution
Participant D — contributed D portion to group solution
Participant E — contributed E portion to group solution
Participant F — contributed F portion to group solution

FIGURE 9.6   Group commitment to the conclusion

her idea has been incorporated into the total group solution. Thus, each member of the group has a personal stake in the success of the group solution.

CONDUCTING A MEETING

We shall consider three main parts of the total meeting process: before the meeting, during the meeting, and after the meeting. As you study the information contained in the following segments, it will become apparent that good meetings do not just happen; they are the result of a great deal of advance planning, hard work, and good personal communication and management skills.

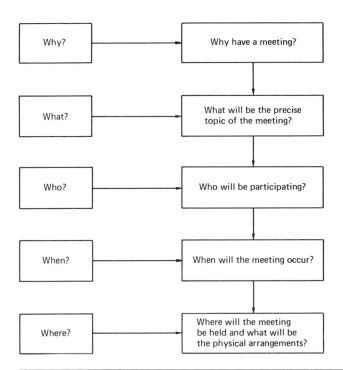

FIGURE 9.7   Premeeting planning model

Before the meeting

We have modified and adapted a premeeting model constructed by Kell and Corts (1980). Figure 9.7 illustrates the planning process.

Why?   Why have a meeting? This is a fundamental question. Many employees are very negative about meetings. They blame countless meetings of little substance or real value for their own personal boredom or lack of productivity. "Oh no, another meeting!" is a common response to the announcement of a meeting. Employees are high-cost entities in a business, and a tremendous amount of financial resources are committed to meetings. If you multiply an individual hourly base salary by the number of people and hours in a given meeting, you will quickly realize how costly the meeting is. To justify the cost, therefore, you must be sure that you really need a meeting.

It is usually helpful for meeting participants to have a thorough understanding of the reason for the meeting. This can be handled in a variety of ways. Figure 9.8 is a sample of an advance notice agenda, which can be circulated to all employees who will be asked to participate in the meeting.

As you will note, the announcement includes a clear statement of the topic for discussion at the meeting. The topic is presented as a question, a format that is discussed elsewhere in this chapter. In addition to the general topic, a specific list of subjects that will be dealt with is included. This list enables those who will be participating in the meeting to prepare adequately in advance for dealing with the specific topic areas. Another piece of information contained in the announcement is an individualized statement about the reasons each person was invited to the meeting. Often these reasons will relate to the person's position in the organization, but they may involve other factors, such as his or her general knowledge and expertise in the field. A final piece of information contained on the announcement form is a list of all those who will be participating in the meeting. Letting everyone know who the other participants will be can reduce participants' anxiety in preparing for the meeting.

There are essentially three purposes for organizing individuals into groups for discussion: fact finding, information sharing, and decision making. These purposes may all be involved and interrelated in any given group discussion. For purposes of elaborating on them and helping you understand the differences between them, however, we will treat them as separate and distinct purposes.

FACT FINDING

Fact-finding discussion occurs for the purpose of discovering or clarifying factual information. A group formed for this purpose is usually given a very specific charge; it frequently has a very narrowly defined subject and a very tight timetable. A group called

MEMO TO: J. T. Fence, Personnel Manager

FROM: C. R. Ports, General Manager

DATE: March 17, 1982

SUBJECT: Conference to review our retirement program

Time and location: April 1, 1982; 1:00-2:30 p.m.; Executive Conference
                     Room

Subject for discussion: Should our company implement survivor benefits as
                          a part of our retirement program?

Main topics for discussion:

          1. Survivor benefits available.

          2. Advantages and disadvantages of such benefits.

          3. Cost for addition of such benefits (start up
             costs).

          4. Long range costs for addition of such benefits.

Reason you are requested to participate:

          As personnel manager, you are familiar with this

          subject from employee criticisms. You are

          knowledgeable about the legal ramifications, pro-

          grams of other companies, and options open to us.

          You will be charged with implementing any

          changes made.

Conference participants (distribution list):

          J. T. Fence   W. M. Grace

          M. E. Mace   E. E. Lahl

          R. Z. Whittier   J. W. Haprish

          J. J. Greenfield   C. C. Apple

FIGURE 9.8   Sample meeting announcement

together for fact-finding purposes may be referred to as a fact-finding team, investigative committee, research team, or similar names.

A fact-finding discussion frequently accomplishes much of its work on an individual basis and relies only minimally on group process. Individual members of the group may be assigned specific aspects of the problem and given the responsibility to research the facts for that narrowly delineated area. The group will get together to hear the results of the investigations of individual members and to help review and clarify points. The group will then put the individual responses and work together into a comprehensive group fact-finding report.

A fact-finding group is usually not a decision-making group in that it usually reports back to the authority that created it. Whatever entity organized the fact-finding group would make any necessary decisions after receiving the report.

INFORMATION SHARING

Information sharing through group discussion occurs when a group meets with the specific purpose of sharing information. This group discussion process is frequently used in business and industry for the purpose of disseminating information informally. In this setting, various members share ideas, information, and perceptions. Formal actions will not necessarily be taken. There are several types of information-sharing groups.

One of the most frequently used types of information-sharing group activity is the *staff meeting*. In this setting, a small group of employees who are assigned together in an office or otherwise administratively organized together within the organization meet to share information and take care of routine business items. The staff meeting usually takes place on a regular basis to provide the opportunity for upward and downward communication. A supervisor can communicate appropriate information to staff members at the same time staff members have an opportunity to communicate ideas to their supervisor. The exchange that occurs in a staff meeting is considered a very positive management tool in maintaining a feeling of open communication.

The *briefing session* is a type of group meeting in which the shared information tends to come from one or a few individuals to the others in the meeting. It is a useful way to disseminate very specific information, and it also can provide an opportunity for a question-and-answer session after the formal presentation of information. Veterans of military service will recall the frequent use of briefing sessions to familiarize servicemen with new procedures, equipment, or orders. A firm that is announcing a new optional insurance program as a part of a fringe benefits package might choose to hold a briefing session to familiarize employees with the program. This meeting might be held in addition to providing written information for each employee. In such a meeting, a representative of the company's personnel office and a representative of the insurance company might make presentations to the group and then open the meeting to discussion and questions.

The *press conference* is a special type of briefing session in which a specific audience group is called together to receive information and to have the opportunity to obtain additional information through questioning. If a new company were moving into the local community, for example, a representative of the company might be invited by the local chamber of commerce to hold a briefing session for other community leaders. At such a meeting, the company representative would be given the opportunity to present basic information concerning the company's plans, such as building plans, number and type of employees, and other related information. City officials, chamber of commerce representatives, and others might also make comments concerning the new company, its value to the local community, and other similar remarks. Others invited to attend would be given an opportunity to ask questions or to make comments concerning the new company. In this way, group discussion occurs in a meeting that was called essentially to share specific information.

In business and industry, sales representatives are frequently called together for *sales meetings*. These meetings may have as their primary purpose the dissemination of information to those responsible for selling a product. The information shared may be in the form of new product information, new marketing information gathered from surveys or other analyses, or information concerning new marketing aids that are being made available to the sales representatives. In the presentation of this information to the sales representatives, all individuals in the meeting have an opportunity to participate by sharing their own information and perspectives and by asking questions for clarification. Here, too, group discussion occurs in a meeting that was called essentially to share information.

DECISION MAKING

Decision-making discussion occurs when a group with the authority to make decisions meets with the express purpose of making a specific decision. This type of group discussion may very well rely on the preliminary work of fact-finding or information-sharing groups. It may be that the decision-making group has already requested a fact-finding report from another subgroup, or perhaps the group has participated in some information-sharing sessions before a session in which it seeks to make a specific decision. This is one way in which the various purposes for group discussion may be interwoven and may overlap. Decision-making group discussion may occur in several different settings.

Decision-making *boards* are usually relatively small groups. We define a board as a group of elected or appointed officials who function collectively as the legal authority for an organization; as such, they are responsible for establishing all policies of the organization. The board of directors of a business or corporation is charged with the ultimate decision-making responsibility. Boards deliberate concerning the policies that should be established and then make a collective decision. The decision made by the group is then passed on to administrative officers for implementation.

A *committee* is usually a subgroup of a larger entity and operates with restricted responsibilities in relation to the parent organization. A company might have committees, for example, on marketing strategy, design, new product development, or safety and health standards. Such committees would have responsibility for those very limited areas and would report recommendations to some larger entity within the corporate body. Final decisions concerning a new marketing strategy, new product development, new safety plan, or other recommendations that might come out of these committees might actually be made by the parent organization, the larger entity in the corporation that created the committee. Committees are useful because they permit small groups of individuals to concentrate on selected problems. This distribution of responsibility and assignment can improve the quality of the recommendations developed within the organization. Such delegation of responsibility to committees is viewed as an efficient method of operation.

A *task force* is a specific subgroup responsible for a special task, usually on an ad hoc basis without any continuing responsibility. In contrast to a committee, which is normally a standing subentity that will have continuing responsibility, a task force is usually assigned a very specific charge to be executed in a limited time frame. It is usually understood that, once the task force has completed its highly specialized work, the task force will be dissolved.

As an example, a valve manufacturing company might have encountered a recurring faulty valve problem in one of its valve mechanism models. The manufacturer might form a task force of engineers representing several different specialty areas to handle the problem—exploring alternative designs for the malfunctioning valve and making recommendations concerning the best solution. Once this specific problem is solved, the task force would be dissolved.

What?   One of the first questions asked in the planning phase should be about the purpose of the meeting. A clear understanding of the purpose is needed by all participants so that they can prepare adequately for effective participation in the group discussion.

If you are slated to participate in a meeting, and you understand the meeting's purpose, you can proceed with preparation. Determine from the information available if the meeting will involve fact finding, information sharing, problem solving, or some combination of these. Analyze the topic in an attempt to subdivide it into its most important parts. In this process you should be able to pinpoint subtopics that will require the gathering of information or additional analytical or creative thinking on your part. Each participant should attempt to have some general information about the whole topic, while seeking to bring his or her own unique strength to the group.

If you are the person doing the initial planning for the group discussion and you will be setting the topic, you may want to keep in mind some helpful ground rules for establishing a topic. It is often considered helpful to phrase the discussion topic in the form of a question. There are three basic types of discussion topic questions: questions of fact, value, or policy.

The *question of fact* is designed to establish truth and assumes that the truth can be known. There may sometimes be a direct yes or no answer to questions of fact. Using the general topic of retirement benefits, for example, a question of fact could be: "Is our retirement program cost effective?" This is a question of fact because established principles of cost effectiveness can be used to determine the factual answer.

The *question of value* seeks to make a relative judgment about a moral, ethical, or other value standard. This type of question explores the goodness or badness, rightness or wrongness of a topic. Again using the topic of retirement benefits as an example, a value question could be: "Is our retirement program, which excludes survivor benefits, morally defensible?" In discussing such a question, group members would be dealing with judgmental issues of right or wrong, based on their own attitudes and feelings.

The *question of policy* attempts to draw out a group's specific recommendation. This type of question usually includes the word *should* in its phrasing. Again using the example of retirement benefits, a question of policy could be: "Should our company implement survivor benefits as a part of our retirement program?" The answer to this question is a judgment that would represent a recommendation from a particular group for policy on that topic.

There tends to be a hierarchy operating with these three types of questions. A question of fact usually will not involve value or policy issues. A question of value may deal with issues of fact but usually not with policy issues. A question of policy may deal with both issues of fact and value.

Who? When considering who will be participating in the meeting, keep in mind that there are essentially two broad categories of individuals who participate in groups. The first is the *task-oriented* individual, a person whose primary concern is the accomplishment of a specific action and who demonstrates little concern for the feelings of the other discussion participants. This type of participant, who is usually very eager to deal with the issues immediately, to solve the problem, and to get to the conclusion part of the discussion, can be somewhat abrasive to other members of the group.

The second type of participant is the *people-oriented* participant, a person whose main concern is for the personal relationships among the various people participating in the group discussion; this person shows minimal concern for accomplishing the group task. This type of individual has a tendency to let the discussion subject or agenda become secondary and to give primary emphasis to the interpersonal relationships among the group members. This type of person feels uneasy trying to bring other group members back into the scheduled agenda and would prefer to let someone get off the track rather than risk hurting feelings by indicating that he or she has gotten off the subject.

In addition to these broad categories of individuals who participate in groups, several other types of people are identifiable at meetings and conferences:

- "Loud Louie" frequently speaks in a loud voice and attempts to dominate the meeting in other ways. This type of individual demonstrates a cocky attitude and a tendency to know it all and has little interest in the opinions and ideas of others.
- "Big Buddy" is the type of participant who—because of physical stature or other factors—has a domineering personality. For some reason, other members of the group seem to be intimidated by this participant, who may speak on

issues with apparently great authority. Such an individual may also have high informal status among peers and is rather automatically revered as a leader.

- "Sour Sam" is very negative and tends to talk against the positions articulated by others at the meeting. This individual has a negative outlook on life, and little that is done by other members of the group will cause him to be more positive.
- "Silent Susie" is usually restrained and quiet throughout the meeting. Even when invited to participate in the discussion, this person may make a very minimal response, answering with a yes or no if at all possible, and it will be difficult to get an elaborate response from her.
- "Gazing Gail" demonstrates a removed attitude and may appear to be daydreaming or gazing, with her thoughts in another world. This type of participant is only minimally involved in the discussion and often makes comments that do not seem to be direct and relevant to the flow of discussion in the meeting.
- "Mumbling Molly" may have some good ideas but has a great deal of difficulty expressing an opinion or communicating effectively. This individual often may rely on "you know," in the hope that other participants will nod their heads and acknowledge that they understand what is being said.

When?   On the meeting announcement that's shown in Figure 9.8, there is a clear indication of the time of the meeting. Not only is the day and hour given, but there is also an indication of the expected duration of the meeting. This courtesy allows people to schedule their other activities around the meeting. Putting parameters on the meeting time also helps participants understand just how detailed the meeting will be. Those who are experienced in conducting meetings have learned how very important it is to set time limits. Without time limits, meetings will tend to be less efficient, more open to extraneous discussion, and less task oriented. Remember that time is money and that everyone's time should be used productively.

Where?   Where a meeting is held may be far more important than most of us are willing to admit. The supervisor who calls subordinates into his or her office for a meeting, for example, may inhibit discussion flow simply because the meeting is located in the supervisor's office. The same type of meeting held in a neutral conference room might allow members to feel more at ease and therefore be more willing to participate in the meeting.

Whatever physical location of the meeting is set, every effort should be made to obtain excellent facilities. Individuals tend to communicate more openly and easily when they are in comfortable surroundings. Information contained in the premeeting checklist (Figure 9.9) will help you ensure that the location has been set up properly.

It is important to consider the size of the room and the size of the group that will be meeting. A large group of people should not be put in too small a room, since close physical proximity of people in a tightly packed room may create some negative feeling. On the other hand, you do not want to put a small group in too large a room because that will tend to make individual participants feel isolated or lonely, which is not conducive to feeling the togetherness of a group. The room should be the right size for the people attending the meeting to feel comfortable and reasonably close-knit, without extremes.

During the meeting

The discussion that occurs in a good meeting does not just happen; it follows a carefully laid out pattern. Just as you would not start on a long automobile trip without mapping out a route of travel, so you should plan the road to take through a meeting to get to your desired conclusion.

The process that is at work throughout a meeting is fluid and moving. Although we cannot stop it or make it static, we can isolate its elements and identify its specific phases. To get the meeting's job accomplished, there are usually two or more separate processes at work. For our purposes here, we will examine two main processes. The *task dimension process* (Figure 9.10)

PREMEETING CHECKLIST FOR PHYSICAL ARRANGEMENTS

	Check When Completed
ROOM	
Reserved	
Tables	
Chairs	
Sign designating room	
Nameplates	
Podium	
Seating arrangement	
AUDIO-VISUAL EQUIPMENT	
Public address system	
Tape recorder	
Microphones	
Chalkboard	
Flip chart	
Overhead transparency projector	
Other projectors	
Television monitor	
Screen	
PRINTED MATERIAL	
Agenda	
Background position papers	
Others	
SUPPLIES FOR PARTICIPANTS	
Writing paper	
Pens	
Chalk	
Felt marking pen	
Ashtray	
Pitchers of ice water/glasses	

FIGURE 9.9   Premeeting checklist for physical arrangements

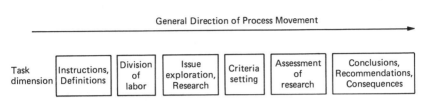

FIGURE 9.10   Task dimension process

relates to accomplishing the specific goal of the meeting. If the meeting topic were a question of fact, for example, such as "Is our retirement program cost effective?" then the task dimension process would represent the phases that would have to be considered to answer the question. The other process is the *social dimension process* (Figure 9.11), which relates to the interpersonal relationships that are customary in a meeting setting. The courtesies expected between participants in a meeting have been codified in the social dimension process.

TASK DIMENSION PROCESS

In the *instructions/definitions* phase of the meeting, the leader has the opportunity to outline any specific instructions to group members and to indicate the general plan intended for the meeting. If an agenda has been prepared, this would be an appropriate time to refer to the agenda or distribute it to any who might need copies. This is also the time for a brief overview of the key elements in the agenda and for definition of any terms that might be unfamiliar to any members of the group.

The *division of labor* phase is a time when the group may decide to divide up the issue under discussion and give certain

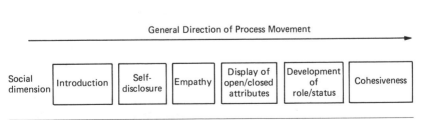

FIGURE 9.11   Social dimension process

members of the group primary responsibility for specific aspects of the topic. Any division of labor that might be helpful to the total group process can occur in this phase of the process.

The *issue exploration/research* phase is the heart of discussion in a meeting. This is a time for members to share their perspectives on the issue and to relate research or information to the other members of the group. Full exploration of issues and sharing of specific research information is important before the group moves toward any conclusions. Many groups do not spend sufficient time on this phase and rush too quickly into conclusions or solutions.

The *criteria setting* phase is when the group should discuss some bases for judging the quality of the conclusions that will be suggested. Establishing guidelines by which the group will judge whether or not a possible conclusion should be accepted will allow a more objective and rational determination of the group conclusion or solution.

The *assessment of research* phase is when the group should begin a critical evaluation of possible conclusions or recommendations that came from the research and issue exploration phase. This assessment process should attempt to evaluate the conclusions and recommendations as they relate to the established criteria.

The *conclusions/recommendations/consequences* phase is when, having established that conclusions and recommendations meet the criteria, the group should consider the possible consequences of conclusions and recommendations.

SOCIAL DIMENSION PROCESS

In the *introduction* phase, courtesy dictates that all those present at a meeting should be introduced, to establish some level of familiarity. In a group meeting at which all members are already well known to one another, this introductory period may be used for informal conversation.

The *self disclosure* phase of a group discussion occurs as members begin to share their personal perspectives on the issues. As a person shares a point of view, he or she is in a sense revealing personal information about beliefs, attitudes, and opinions. This sharing of information that reflects personal attributes, known as self-disclosure, is a healthy second phase in the social dimension process.

The *empathy* phase occurs when members demonstrate a feeling of togetherness or oneness. Relating or identifying with other group members creates a positive feeling of group identity. It is important for a group to develop this empathy in order to achieve a feeling of group unity.

The *open/closed attributes* phase occurs in the process of analyzing the issues and considering possible conclusions and solutions, when individuals within the group display either open attitudes, indicating a willingness both to accept the positions of others and to alter their own positions, or closed attitudes, demonstrating a lack of willingness to change or alter their positions.

The *development of role or status* of individual members in a group may change during the course of the meeting as individuals contribute to the group process. Some members may have had predetermined status, based on their position in the organization or their familiarity with other members of the group.

As a group shares in the interaction of oral communication, a feeling of *cohesiveness* should develop by which individual feelings become subservient to a group awareness and a group feeling. This cohesiveness, when or if it occurs, is a high point of the social process development.

We usually think of evaluation as occurring after the fact. Although we will discuss evaluation as part of the next section, "After the Meeting," participants in a discussion should be sensitive to evaluating the process while the meeting is in progress. This in-progress evaluation is known as *formative evaluation*. Since many business meetings are problem-solving meetings, we shall consider an example of formative evaluation applied to the problem-solving process. The model shown in Figure 9.12 will give you an idea of the elements involved in formative evaluation.

As the process proceeds from phase to phase, such as from definition to problem exploration, group members should evaluate whether or not the first phase of the process has been handled adequately before moving to the next phase. This evaluation should be continuous as the group moves from phase to phase.

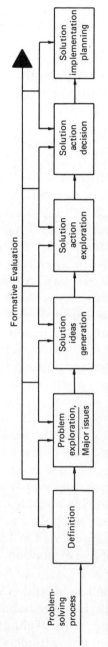

FIGURE 9.12 Model of formative evaluation applied to the problem-solving process

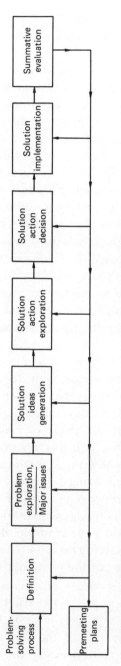

FIGURE 9.13 Model of summative evaluation applied to the problem-solving process

After the meeting

We sometimes have a tendency to breathe a sigh of relief and relax after a meeting, as if we were happy just to have made it through the meeting alive. This is especially true following the vigorous group discussions that can take place in the highly competitive business world. Nevertheless, a meeting should be evaluated carefully after its conclusion.

It is sometimes helpful to allow a brief time to elapse between the conclusion of the meeting and any effort to evaluate it. You should be careful, however, not to allow too much time to elapse, because your recall of the events will begin to fade. As a general rule, about a one-day lapse is sufficient time to give you some perspective.

Although each participant in the meeting may do a personal evaluation, the primary evaluation should be conducted by the person who proposed the meeting. At this point a *summative* evaluation is in order. Recalling the model for formative evaluation, a similar model can be used for a summative evaluation of the problem-solving process. Figure 9.13 shows that this evaluation, which is done after some time has elapsed following the conclusion of the meeting, considers each phase of the problem-solving process. The evaluation also goes back to the premeeting planning, at which time the objectives of the meeting were articulated. Summative evaluation thus considers whether the purposes of the meeting were fulfilled.

After the meeting, you should summarize the entire meeting in written form. This summary is sometimes referred to as *minutes* for standing organizations, but for business conferences and meetings a more appropriate term is *summary of meeting*. This written summary will assist you in your analysis and evaluation of the meeting, to determine if you were successful in accomplishing the objectives for which the meeting was called.

It is very appropriate to circulate a summary of the meeting to all participants. Also, if any action occurred as a result of the meeting, it is a courtesy to advise the participants that specific action did result from the meeting. By taking a little time to accomplish these courtesies, you will help reduce the frustration of staff

MEMO TO: J. T. Fence, Personnel Manager

FROM: C. R. Ports, General Manager

DATE: April 2, 1982

SUBJECT: Summary of conference reviewing our retirement program;
            conference held April 1, 1982, 1:00–2:30 p.m.; Executive Con-
            ference Room

Summary of main points discussed:

1. _____

2. _____

3. _____

4. _____

5. _____

6. _____

Follow-up required:

1. J. T. Fence: _____

_____

2. E. E. Lahl: _____

_____

3. R. Z. Whittier: _____

_____

Conference participants (distribution list):

J. T. Fence	W. M. Grace
M. E. Mace	E. E. Lahl
R. Z. Whittier	H. W. Haprish
J. J. Greenfield	C. C. Apple

FIGURE 9.14   Sample meeting summary

members who participate in the meetings. Many employees feel that meetings are a waste of time, but obtaining the summary and an indication of action will help reduce their frustration level. Figure 9.14 is a sample summary format.

SUMMARY

This chapter stressed the important role of group discussion in meetings and conferences of the business world. Specific ways in which business uses groups were identified. The group discussion that occurs in business meetings was identified as a process, and various strengths in using the group process were elaborated.

Conducting meetings was viewed as a three part process. Discussion of preparation before the meeting included consideration of such items as the meeting purpose, the meeting type (fact finding, information sharing, or decision making), the meeting topic phrased as a question, the kinds of people who participate in meetings, procedural matters, and planning of physical arrangements. In the section "During the meeting," the part of the process identified as the heart of the meeting, we covered the two major dimensions of the group process—the task dimension and the social dimension. Evaluation of the effectiveness of the meetings was discussed as a responsibility after the meeting.

EXERCISES

1. Create fictitious information for a meeting that you are setting up and conducting. Prepare an announcement for the meeting and a postmeeting summary. Follow the formats outlined in this chapter.
2. Divide the class into approximately equal groups of five to seven students. Each group should select a topic and conduct a discussion in front of the class while other class members observe.
3. Write a brief critique of the discussions conducted in class as part of exercise 2. Prepare either a general evaluation or specific evaluations of certain social or task functions, using

the phases in Figure 9.10 for the task dimension and Figure 9.11 for the social dimension.

REFERENCES AND SUGGESTED READINGS

Bormann, Ernest G., and Bormann, Nancy C. 1972. *Effective Small Group Communication*. Minneapolis: Burgess.

Cartwright, Dorwin, and Zander, Alan. 1968. *Group Dynamics: Research and Theory*, 3rd ed. New York: Harper & Row.

Golde, Roger A. 1972. "Are Your Meetings Like This One?," *Harvard Business Review* 50:68.

Gulley, Halbert S., and Leathers, Dale G. 1977. *Communication and Group Process*, 3rd ed. New York: Holt, Rinehart and Winston.

Huseman, Richard C., Logue, Cal M., and Freshley, Dwight L., eds. *Reading in Interpersonal and Organizational Communication*, 3rd ed. Boston: Holbrook.

Kell, Carl L., and Corts, Paul R. 1980. *Fundamentals of Effective Group Communication*. New York: Macmillan.

O'Connor, J. Regis. 1978. "Communicating in Groups." In Randall Capps and J. Regis O'Connor, eds, *Fundamentals of Effective Speech Communication*. Cambridge, Mass.: Winthrop.

Sigband, Norman B. 1976. *Communication for Management and Business*, 2nd ed. Glenview, Ill.: Scott, Foresman (especially "Readings in Communication").

Smith, William S. 1965. *Group Problem Solving Through Discussion*, rev. ed. Indianapolis: Bobbs Merrill.

Tubbs, Stewart L. 1978. *A Systems Approach to Small Group Interaction*. Reading, Mass.: Addison-Wesley.

Chapter 10

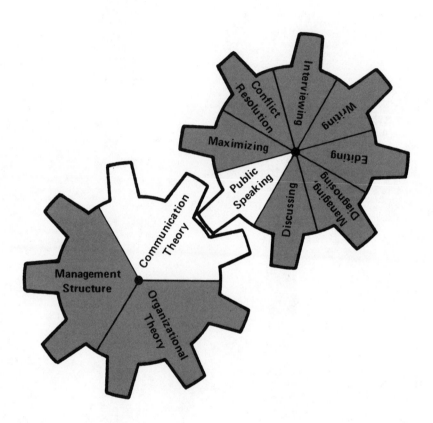

"Today, I'd Like to Talk About..."
SKILLS IN PUBLIC COMMUNICATION

This chapter will provide you with the following:

1. an understanding of the general nature of the speech audience and how to select a topic for them

2. the ability to collect speech information and subsequently prepare a speech purpose

3. the ability to practice, polish, and deliver your speech according to the suggestions and adjustments listed here

4. the ability to prepare an informative and persuasive speech with the preparation guides and examples given here

The three-phase career chart in Chapter 3 argues that public speaking is the communication skill in greatest demand and the primary communication skill in training seminars in phases I, II, and III. We do not intend to imply that, in phase I (entry level to 5 years), you should wait several years until someone asks you to speak in a business or social setting. On the contrary, public communication skills should rank high on your list of job and career priorities, along with the obvious interpersonal skills you will need to master. We believe that an entry level employee with even minimal public speaking competences may have a special edge that will help to obtain a better position with greater opportunities for advancement. A well-rounded employee with the ability to deliver a variety of speeches is a unique asset to his or her company.

In this chapter, we will provide a summary of basic principles of public communication in business and organizational settings. We will discuss public communication, its person-to-person character, and what we consider seven basic truths about contemporary business and community audiences. We will cover informative and persuasive speaking, presenting two guides for preparation and delivery. Finally, we will recommend a prescriptive list of do's and don't's for effective public communication.

PUBLIC COMMUNICATION: TALKING PERSON TO PERSON

Speeches are given because audiences exist. Today's audiences are looking for information, entertainment, reinforcement of accepted ideas, and for critical listening concerning themes that may change their attitudes, opinions, and even behavior. Public communication is valued and used frequently by every organization to fulfill important purposes. Whether inside or outside the work place, a speaker assumes complete responsibility for designing and delivering a message to a group of interested people. Among the various settings for speeches are a variety of internal business settings and community settings, including the following:

In-house speech settings
- supervisory or management meetings on company policies and practices
- organizational meetings with department directors
- picnics, plant parties, awards banquets, and seminar sessions
- technical presentations
- briefing and orientation sessions
- training programs and seminars
- end-of-year reports by company leaders
- persuasive-sessions concerning productivity or correction of low employee output

Community settings
- social club presentations
- convention or conference presentations
- formal public speeches concerning a company's civic responsibilities and the like
- a formal speaker's bureau to acquaint the community with an organization's services

In our society, business and industry use public communication because the free enterprise system is based on several basic human interests, such as:

- How can we convince our customers that we are deeply interested in their desires to obtain a good product or service for a noninflationary price?
- How can we overcome public fears that our products or services are unfairly priced?
- How can we get our public to see the comparative value of our products or services over their current spending habits?
- How can we get our public to act responsibly when faced with the widespread need to reduce personal consumption of resources to leave enough for all to use?

Wide World Photos

Public communication is a survival skill of business life

The list could go on. Sooner or later, all these business concerns require an internal or external public speaking event to present the best and most informed thoughts of key personnel to employees or the community. You may become a public speaker for your company, whether you like the idea or not.

Rather than learning to live with a possibly undesirable task, you should examine, with great care, the person-to-person dimensions of public speaking and find out for yourself what you should know to be prepared to "give a little talk." As you read, listen, and critique the public speakers around you, you will discover seven basic truths about the dynamics of public speaking:

1. Today's sophisticated audiences expect a speaker to present a planned set of ideas that are easily remembered and are developed into solid informational patterns or arguments.
2. Today's audiences will not accept appeals based solely on emotional or personal attacks.
3. Today's audiences expect to be talked with, not addressed oratorically.
4. Today's audiences are open to new ideas, change, and progress, as well as the more traditional concerns for safety, conservation, and the qualities of "the good old days."
5. Today's audiences will not tolerate a poorly prepared speaker or speech.
6. Today's audiences reserve the right to accept or reject the purpose of a speaker and his speech. In short, the freedom of speech also includes the freedom to listen.
7. Finally, members of today's audiences always consider themselves *individuals*. You must learn what your publics think about the issues in your field, what people are thinking and saying about your business organization. You must read and learn all you can about people. A wise businessman once remarked that, when a public speaker can give his audience what they want, he will have become a successful public servant for his business or organization.

From years of public and private speech communication and business communication instruction, we are convinced that public speaking is a person-to-person encounter whereby a speaker acquires the most valuable lessons of human dynamics. As part of the communication skills cycle, public speaking training and experience can be very important for a business because of the public's continuing need to know and business's continuing need to say. In short, today's business community needs people who can give public speeches.

Informative and persuasive speaking are the two major forms

used in business and community situations. We have prepared a guide for each type of activity, and we have selected the major elements from each guide for discussion and detail.

SPEAKING TO INFORM

It is likely that your early public communication appearances will be for informative rather than persuasive purposes. As you grow in respect, career advancement, and tenure with a business, it is more likely that you will be called upon to give a persuasive speech. With that division in mind, we will discuss the three major forms of informative discourse: explaining, technical briefing, and informing.

For both business and community purposes, speaking to *explain* requires that the speaker prepare *short* units of material to be followed by direct or indirect feedback from the audience. If the company sick leave policy, for example, has five major clauses, it would be sensible to check with the listeners after explaining each part to measure their comprehension. If audience understanding of the parts is possible, then understanding of the entire message is probable.

An organization always benefits when all of its members understand their roles, tasks, and responsibilities. As listener comprehension is the objective of *technical briefing*, a supervisor, manager, or executive may prepare a speech and visual presentation to highlight the major information required by the audience. In the presentation, specific units of questions and answers can be designed for listener comprehension.

A speech to *inform* may also carry goodwill, cordial thanks for past favors, subtle responses to community distrust, and so on. Generally, an informative talk in the public arena has data to share at one level, but goodwill is at the core of its purpose. In this respect, the thin line between informative and persuasive speeches is often blurred. Still, all organizations require information for their continued existence. You will be called upon to share your ideas, report on the progress of a mission, instruct others in job-related policies, and a variety of other assignments. You must be sure that your informational talk is accurate, complete, contemporary, and understandable. That is all an audience can expect.

Figure 10.1 presents a guide for informative speaking. You can use this guide in preparing for in-class informative speeches by checking off each item as you complete it. From the preparation guide we see that there are nine main steps in speech preparation:

1. selecting a suitable topic
2. analyzing your audience
3. collecting information
4. selecting a speech focus
5. organizing the speech
6. selecting the speech content
7. practicing the speech
8. polishing the speech
9. delivering the speech

Steps 1 and 2 overlap, because the audience determines the speech topic. Steps 3, 4, 5, and 6 also overlap, since organizing a speech involves selecting information to be used in the speech; and steps 7, 8, and 9 overlap, since practicing a speech results in more polished style and delivery.

With the guide in mind, we will discuss (1) selecting a topic and analyzing the audience; (2) collecting speech information and selecting the speech focus and content; (3) organizing the speech body, introduction, and conclusion; and (4) practicing, polishing, and delivering the speech.

Selecting a topic and analyzing the audience

You will be asked to give a talk or a public speech only when someone believes that you have something to say that is worth hearing or that you have special knowledge that an audience needs to hear. With your topic already selected for you, your real need as a speaker is to understand the nature of your audience. Quite simply, that means being able to predict with some accuracy the responses of your audience to you and your speech before, during, and after the speech.

1. Selecting suitable topic
   Based on:

   _____ 1.1 Own interests

   _____ 1.2 Audience interests, knowledge, and expectations

   _____ 1.3 Speaking situation

   _____ 1.4 Availability of resources and preparation time

   Topic selected: _____

2. Analyzing audience and situation

   _____ 2.1 Assesses type of situation (e.g., degree of formality, audience expectations)

   _____ 2.2 Assesses probable degree of audience interest in topic:
   Highly   Highly
   uninterested _____ : _____ : _____ : interested

   _____ 2.3 Assesses probable degree of audience knowledge of topic:
   Highly   Highly
   uninformed _____ : _____ : _____ : informed

   Description of audience and situation:

3. Collecting data (taking a clear picture of reality).

   _____ 3.1 Takes stock of own knowledge on subject

   _____ 3.2 Examines several authoritative sources (e.g., through reading, interviewing, listening to speeches, etc.).

   Annotated bibliography:

4. Selecting focus statement

   _____ 4.1 Summarizes central idea of potential speech in one sentence.

   _____ 4.2 Properly limits topic in terms of audience level of knowledge and time speech should last

   _____ 4.3 Is directed toward speaker, not the audience.

   _____ 4.4 Subject of focus statement contains the speech topic, and predicate says something about the speech topic

FIGURE 10.1   Preparation guide: informative speech

Example: Bad focus statement: "I intend to explain to you the duties of the typical bank president."

Good focus statement: "The main duty of the typical bank president is to maintain good public relations with his customers."

Your focus statement: _____

_____

5. Carefully organizing the speech

_____ 5.1 Introduction makes audience want to listen to speech

_____ 5.2 Introduction clearly previews main points of speech

_____ 5.3 Body arranged according to a simple pattern
Pattern selected: _____

_____ 5.4 No more than five main points, each of which supports focus statement

_____ 5.5 Each main point backed by supporting materials that clarify the meaning of the point to audience

_____ 5.6 Transitions help audience keep up with the speaker

_____ 5.7 Conclusion reviews main points of speech

_____ 5.8 Speech closes with memorable statement

6. Selecting speech content

_____ 6.1 Main idea and supporting main points adapted to audience and situation

_____ 6.2 Supporting materials new and significant to audience and logically sound

_____ 6.3 Includes variety of supporting materials.
Types used:

_____ Examples		_____ Statistics	
_____ Analogies		_____ Quotations	
_____ Visual aids		_____ Explanation	
_____ Other (name them: _____)			

continued

FIGURE 10.1 Continued

_____ 6.4 Includes attention factors

Type used:

_____ Shock technique   _____ Contrast

_____ Movement and change   _____ Repetition

_____ Proximity   _____ Intensity

_____ Novelty   _____ Stories

_____ Other (name them: _____)

_____ 6.5 Provides intermittent rest periods (e.g., through occasional humor, restatement, slowing of rate)

_____ 6.6 Comes down out of clouds, utilizes concreteness of language

7. Practicing the speech

_____ 7.1 Practices the speech aloud in a voice to be used during actual delivery

_____ 7.2 Times the speech during each trial run

_____ 7.3 Practices contracting and expanding each main point in order to be ready to respond to audience feedback

_____ 7.4 Spreads out practice sessions over several days

8. Polishing the speech

_____ 8.1 Practices speech until the sequence of ideas is well in mind

_____ 8.2 Tapes speech and listens to a recording to see if the language:

_____ is informal (e.g., contains contractions and pronouns)

_____ contains questions

_____ is direct and economical

_____ is concrete

_____ 8.3 Tries speech out on a friend to help determine whether language is clear

9. Delivering the speech

_____ 9.1 Approaches podium with confidence

_____ 9.2 Establishes eye contact before speaking

FIGURE 10.1 Continued

_____ 9.3 Maintains eye contact and adjusts to any negative feedback

_____ 9.4 Avoids using a manuscript or memorized delivery

_____ 9.5 Speaks in conversational tone of voice

_____ 9.6 Allows content of speech to govern changes in rate, volume, and pitch

_____ 9.7 Speaks loudly enough to be heard

_____ 9.8 Pronounces correctly and enunciates clearly

_____ 9.9 Avoids "uh," "like," "and uh," "you know," or any combination of these verbalized pauses

_____ 9.10 Stands comfortably, allowing freedom to gesture or move about

_____ 9.11 Avoids distracting mannerisms, such as pacing, playing with notes, frequent shifting of stance, etc.

_____ 9.12 Focuses own attention on sharing the information with audience

_____ 9.13 Maintains emotional contact—rapport—with audience

_____ 9.14 Finishes speech, then leaves podium with confidence

FIGURE 10.1 Continued

Whatever topic you intend to share with the audience, you must realize that every member of your audience will have a different attitude toward the topic and your purpose. If the audience feels warmly toward you and your speech, you will have an attentive response. If either you or your topic causes strong negative reactions, you will have a serious problem in achieving your purposes.

Before every speech occasion, large or small, you should make some precise decisions about how much or how little you wish to give your audience in the speech time allotted. As mentioned earlier, an audience has some expectations about you and your topic before and while they listen. Also, remember that an audience will not give you nearly as much attention as you give them, but they will listen only as well or as poorly as you speak. In every regard, you are in control of the public speaking event. Your audience generally will grant you their eyes and ears, but you must constantly monitor their behavior so that you do not lose your way and are not ceremoniously rejected.

Collecting speech information and selecting its focus

You are your own best source of speech ideas and information. Your statements about what you know, feel, or have seen or read are your strongest means for holding the attention of your audience. Next come library materials, trade journals, and audiovisual materials needed to support your ideas.

Having gathered enough materials to go well beyond the allotted time, you must select and phrase a speech focus that captures the reason you are speaking and what will be accomplished when the audience has heard the speech. When you have an eight- to ten-word simple statement of the speech focus, you can organize the speech into major points and supporting detail.

Organizing the speech

The speech body   The following outline needs refinement, but it is essentially a *speech*—a collected set of ideas arranged for the listeners. (For detailed guidelines for outlining a speech, see Appendix E.)

EMPLOYEE INVESTMENT IN COMPANY STOCK

   I. The nature of employee investment programs: "Today, I am going to discuss the employee investment plan at Tabor, Inc. by looking at (1) its main themes, (2) its conceptual foundations, and (3) its limitless future."
   A. What is it?
   B. Who is using the plan today?
      1. Turner Industries
      2. Union Underwear
      3. Visorin, Inc.
      4. B. J., Inc.
   C. What are the employee obligations in the plan?

II. Conceptual foundation of employee investment
 A. Why allow workers to invest?
 B. The need to hold onto company employees
 C. Providing the company with a solid investment portfolio
III. Its limitless future
 A. Workers have a hedge against their inflated budgets by investment.
 B. Workers pass along their savings to their families.
 C. Workers encourage other good workers in other similar jobs to join them in their organization.

The introduction   As noted earlier, the introduction and conclusion of a speech are the last items to be prepared in the speech plan. You already have a ready storehouse of materials to introduce or conclude your speech. You might select, for example, a humorous story from the speech subject, a set of dazzling facts pinpointing the main issue, or various figures of speech that capture the audience's immediate attention and maintain subsequent interest.

A good rule of thumb of introduction planning is to select the best language tool that quickly locks in the audience. An audience will tune out a speaker early in a speech if they are sure that he or she does not care if they listen or not. Thus, the introduction of your speech should generally include the following elements:

1. an attention-getting device
2. a subject-related series of comments that introduces the topic to be shared
3. a purpose sentence that tells the audience, with some precision, specifically what the speaker has chosen to discuss about the topic
4. an opening summary of the major headings of the speech in the order in which they will appear.

An example of a good introduction is as follows:

In today's paper, it was announced that the Viadode Company has established new employee safety policies to offset federal investigations into recent plant shutdowns. In the face of recessionary influences on product profit and loss reports, it is important for Viadode Company employees to be aware of the new safety policies and the resulting impact on the company's immediate future.

With that knotty problem in mind, I'd like to discuss the Viadode Company policy on employee safety and the financial results of improved personal security on the job. To accomplish my purpose, I will discuss two major subjects: (1) the current Viadode safety policies and the new changes in those policies, and (2) the expected improvements to the Viadode financial profile as a natural result of these new safety policies.

In any speech situation, the circumstances surrounding the speech event, the nature of the audience, the difficulty of the speech material, and so on, help determine the length of the speech introduction. It is advisable to keep the introduction within two to three minutes, regardless of how short or long the speech will be. Remember, the introduction needs to accomplish only four structural objectives. The more quickly and accurately an introduction meets its obligations, the sooner the real reason for the public occasion—the speech itself—can be initiated.

The conclusion The purpose of a conclusion is to put an end to the speech. A well-developed conclusion will summarize the major points, deliver a clinching appeal, and pull together all the speech's ideas into a final, fresh understanding for the audience to take away with them.

An example of a good conclusion is as follows:

By now, you can see that the Viadode Company "looked the other way" for years on the subject of plant safety and security. The federal government eventually called our hand on these matters, and the rest is history. History can repeat itself, but, as I have explained, (1) we have set in motion new safety measures as standard policies, and (2) we believe that your improved work place will provide financial rewards for us all in improved salaries and product sales. Saying you are sorry is not enough. The Viadode Company joins hands with you in a common bond to make our future as bright as our past has been dark.

Practicing, polishing, and delivering the speech

A vast majority of business speeches are extemporaneous —carefully prepared, but not memorized, and given from notes but not read. Although several methods of note preparation and use will work, we suggest the following:

1. Write the main units of your speech—phrases or sentences—on large note cards.
2. Do not hide the cards while you speak. Use them as you gesture if it will help.
3. Number your cards in colored ink so that you can keep them in order easily.
4. Use different ink colors for major and minor points.
5. Put as little speech material on your cards as possible so that you can converse with your audience rather than read to them.
6. Be sure to use your cards. Rely on them for direction and control of the message. Underreliance might indicate that you are not prepared.

Extemporaneous speaking requires that you maintain a variety of contacts with your audience, including the following:

- *Eye contact:* This involves watching people as they are responding to your ideas and nonverbal messages. When you practice, imagine seeing members of your audience, and your actual speech will be more personal and direct.
- *Ear contact:* If you cannot be heard by people in the back row, there is no sense in speaking.
- *Idea contact:* Is your topic connecting with your audience? Have you selected the right words, examples, and so on, to gain and maintain their attention?
- *Speech contact:* Have you set the speech into a flow and tempo of delivery whereby the audience does not get ahead of you or get lost behind your speech outline? Tempo is an important consideration that takes into account every aspect of public communication. It is not an easy concept to explain, but your instructor is well versed in it and will help you work on tempo.

As you progress in the study of public communication you will encounter a number of questions that focus on the communication dimensions of public speaking. These questions need answers. The following list provides some simple guidelines for extemporaneous speaking. Study them well and learn to use them.

1. Use *examples, examples,* and more *examples* in your speech.
2. If possible, begin your speech with a personal experience.
3. Speak with ideas, not with words.
4. Use exhibits whenever possible. The chalkboard is a good visual aid.
5. Use variety in your speech.
6. Speak loudly enough to be heard comfortably and slowly enough to be understood.
7. Talk to the group as you would to one individual.
8. Appeal to the listeners' soft spots—money, home, love, patriotism.
9. Use well-structured, grammatical sentences.
10. Look at your listeners—and really see them—all the time.
11. Don't let your speech sound like a speech.
12. Have a real desire to communicate; enjoy the speech yourself.
13. Compliment your audience about something if you can.
14. Put your audience at ease. Be at ease yourself.
15. Be genial, cheerful, confident, animated, brisk, and sincere.
16. Be yourself. Put your own personality into your delivery.
17. Discuss your speech with your friends in order to gain greater familiarity with it.
18. Deal with only subjects about which you have a sizable knowledge or about which you are vitally concerned.
19. Memorize the first part of the introduction and the last part of the conclusion.
20. Slow down your normal speaking rate while delivering the speech.
21. Prepare in advance. If you count on inspiration, you can expect trouble.
22. Make sure that your opinions and beliefs are based on authority and facts.

23. Enliven the speech and stimulate the audience by using figures of speech.
24. Be enthusiastic. Your audience will forgive you almost every fault if you are enthusiastic.
25. Use humor frequently but only to illustrate a point.
26. Never tell off-color stories. Even those who like them will not appreciate it.

SPEAKING TO PERSUADE

Responsible persuasive speech communication is more than just mouthing jargon. A salesman's speech is but one of the forms of speech communication aimed at attitude formation and action. In business, you may be called upon to sell a proposal to your immediate supervisor, to motivate an office staff to greater efficiency or productivity, or to sell a community audience on a change in business procedures that affects that larger audience.

Figure 10.2 presents a preparation guide for persuasive speaking. Use this guide in preparing for in-class persuasive speeches by checking each item as you complete it.

To speak persuasively, you must reveal your qualifications, your goodwill, your expertise, and your trustworthiness. You must bring your credibility and your good reputation with you when you go to speak.

You must also make your ideas credible by citing outside sources that explain, solidify factually, or testify to the points you are making. Supporting materials can be classified as either *artistic* or *inartistic*. Artistic proofs are those types of support that a speaker creates—that is, emotional or ethical proofs—while inartistic proofs are those from outside sources.

Such outside sources as statistical information, expert testimony, concrete examples, and illustrations require careful interpretation and proper use in a persuasive speech. Specifically, you should first be certain that the material proves your point to a reasonable degree, secure enough for audience acceptance. Simply ask yourself: "Does the material I am using support the claim I am making in my argument?" If not, find better evidence. Second,

1. Selecting suitable topic
   Based on:

   _____ 1.1 Own interests

   _____ 1.2 Topic significance.

   _____ 1.3 Audience attitudes, interest, knowledge, and expectations

   _____ 1.4 Speaking situation

   _____ 1.5 Availability of resources and preparation time.

   Topic selected: _____

2. Analyzing audience and situation

   _____ 2.1 Assesses type of situation

   _____ 2.2 Assesses probable audience attitudes on topic.

   Indicate probable attitudes: _____
   _____

   _____ 2.3 Assesses probable audience interest in topic.
   Highly   Highly
   uninterested _____ : _____ : _____ : interested

   _____ 2.4 Assesses probable degree of audience knowledge of topic.
   Highly   Highly
   uninformed _____ : _____ : _____ : informed

3. Collecting data (taking a clear picture of reality)

   _____ 3.1 Assesses own attitudes on topic
   Indicate what filters might make it difficult for you to take a
   clear picture of reality:

   _____ 3.2 Takes stock of own knowledge on topic

   _____ 3.3 Examines sources representing all major viewpoints on
   topic

   _____ 3.4 Scrutinizes logic of every source.

   Annotated bibliography:

FIGURE 10.2   Preparation guide: persuasive speech (proposing a change)

4. Selecting focus statement

      _____ 4.1 Presents a proposition of policy summarizing the solution advocated in the speech (e.g., "Marijuana should be legalized")

      _____ 4.2 Sets up a realistic goal for persuading the audience

Your focus statement: _____

Probable range of audience attitudes toward policy advocated in focus statement:

Strongly   Strongly
Negative _____ : _____ : _____ : _____ : _____ : _____ : Positive

5. Carefully organizing speech.

      _____ 5.1 Introduction makes audience want to listen to speech

      _____ 5.2 Contains no more than five main points

      _____ 5.3 Each main point sufficiently supported to be convincing to the audience

      _____ 5.4 Organization chosen on basis of audience analysis

      _____ 5.5 Transitions help audience keep up

      _____ 5.6 Conclusion motivates audience to take action

6. Selecting speech content

      _____ 6.1 Content probably interesting to audience

      _____ 6.2 Content probably convincing to audience

      _____ 6.3 Content probably impelling to audience

      _____ 6.4 Assertions backed up logically

      _____ 6.5 Includes variety of supporting materials

      _____ 6.6 Includes attention factors

      _____ 6.7 Provides intermittent rest periods

continued

FIGURE 10.2 Continued

_____ 6.8 Is not all on same level of emotional intensity

_____ 6.9 Comes down out of clouds, utilizes concreteness of language

7. Practicing the speech

_____ 7.1 Practices speech aloud in voice to be used during actual delivery

_____ 7.2 Times speech during each trial run

_____ 7.3 Practices contracting and expanding each main point in order to be ready to respond to audience feedback

_____ 7.4 Spreads practice sessions over several days

8. Polishing the speech

_____ 8.1 Practices speech until the sequence of ideas is well in mind

_____ 8.2 Tapes the speech and listens to a recording to see if the language:
  _____ contains no words that would turn off audience
  _____ is informal
  _____ contains questions
  _____ is direct and economical
  _____ is concrete

_____ 8.3 Tries speech out on a friend to help determine whether language is clear

9. Delivering the speech

_____ 9.1 Approaches podium with confidence

_____ 9.2 Establishes eye contact before speaking

_____ 9.3 Maintains eye contact and adjusts to any negative feedback

_____ 9.4 Avoids using manuscript or memorized delivery

_____ 9.5 Speaks in conversational tone of voice

_____ 9.6 Allows content of speech to govern changes in rate, volume, and pitch

FIGURE 10.2   Continued

_____ 9.7 Speaks loudly enough to be heard

_____ 9.8 Pronounces correctly and enunciates clearly

_____ 9.9 Avoids "uh," "like," "and uh, " "you know," or any combination of these verbalized pauses

_____ 9.10 Stands comfortably, allowing freedom to gesture or move
about

_____ 9.11 Avoids distracting mannerisms, such as pacing, playing
with notes, frequent shifting of stance, etc.

_____ 9.12 Focuses own attention on persuading and motivating audience

_____ 9.13 Talks with, not at, audience

_____ 9.14 Maintains emotional contact with audience

_____ 9.15 Finishes speech, then leaves podium with confidence

FIGURE 10.2 Continued

you should simplify your use of statistics, quotations, and the like. When in doubt, trim your sources to a precious few. Be on guard against overkill by using long lists of quoted items. Finally, you should vary the kinds of supporting material to prove your points. You will be the benefactor of a speech that covers all the bases, avoiding the monotony of one kind of evidence.

Figure 10.3 is an example of an effective persuasive speech—a student oration on auto safety—that is included here to illustrate the speaker's plan and the measures taken to make her ideas credible with outside sources that testify to the points in the speech. The speeches in the Appendixes A through C are similar. Each speech is constructed with the previously explained variety of proofs—that is, personal testimony, statistical data, and emotional appeals. Study these speeches as you prepare your own speeches. These excellent examples will provide ideas and techniques that will assist you when you are asked to "give a little talk."

STUDENT ANALYSIS

STUDENT SPEECH

YOUR FRIENDLY
NEIGHBORHOOD MECHANIC
Deadra Longworth

Mankato State University

Mankato, Minnesota

Coached by Larry Schnoor

Uses two personal experiences to introduce topic. They are realistic enough to gain attention and yet surprising enough to arouse interest in causes and solutions.	Last March while driving home on Interstate 80, I suddenly realized that even though I was applying pressure to my gas pedal, I was going nowhere. Fortunately, I was able to pull off the freeway, down an exit ramp and anxiously into an awaiting service station. After the mechanic checked the car over, he assured me, "Don't worry little lady, you only have a broken fan belt." Well, this "little lady" left Iowa owing a bill of $85.00 for the replacement of that broken fan belt.
Ethical appeals supporting speaker credibility through personal examples	Last October 23, I rode with a group of students to Omaha, Nebraska, in a large van. Later that evening as one of the students was returning home from his night on the town, he suddenly lost his ability to shift. He was lucky that he was not injured, but his speed was slow enough so he could pull off to the side of the road and wait to be towed to a garage. Believe me, it was difficult for him to accept the bill of $375.00 when you consider that just a week before he had paid $285.00 for a new rebuilt transmission.
Transition	Instances like this can happen to anybody at any time, but both of my cases involve a common denomination: auto repair incompetency and fraud.

FIGURE 10.3 Sample persuasive speech

Speech reprinted from *Winning Orations* (Mankato, Minn.: The Interstate Oratorical Association, 1976). Reprinted by permission.

STUDENT ANALYSIS	STUDENT SPEECH
Rhetorical questions are then asked for application of problems to the audience. It might stimulate the listeners to think of other similar personal experiences which yielded a comparable result.	When was the last time you had your car in the garage for repairs? Were you pleased with the work that was done? Do you believe you were treated honestly and fairly? That the price you were charged was relatively just? Well if you were, please leave me the name of the mechanic. Unfortunately, most of us leave these service stations feeling totally frustrated and upset.

Problem ⟶ Owning an automobile may be the American dream, but keeping it repaired has become the American nightmare.

Good contrast between "dream" and "nightmare."

Supplementing every man's personal experience, evidence exists to show that the incompetency and fraud of the Auto Repair Industry can no longer be ignored and that steps must be taken to correct this abuse of the driving public. This abuse involves inflated costs, deceitful practices, and inexcusable incompetency.

Introduces three problem areas.

PROBLEMS
A. Inflated costs:

Expert opinion

Statistics

Popular Science states that last year inadequate auto repair was the leading consumer complaint in America, and Margaret Carlson, former research associate for the Center of Auto Safety, states in her book, How to Get Your Car Repaired Without Getting Gypped, that Americans spend over 29 billion dollars a year on servicing and repair. Yet 11 billion, or almost half, is spent on shoddy, unneeded, and overpriced repairs.

Transition ⟶ Now, many bad repairs can be attributed to incompetency, but plenty are

B. Fraud: outrageous frauds that contribute heavily to the wasted 11 billion a year.

continued

FIGURE 10.3   Continued

STUDENT ANALYSIS

STUDENT SPEECH

Expert opinion

Hypothetical illustration

Transition

Automotive transmissions capable of running 150,000 miles with relatively little maintenance seem to be the most popular target of the dishonest mechanic. In a recent crackdown on transmission rip-off, the U.S. Attorney's office in Washington, D.C., uncovered a modus operandi typical of many crooked shops. It goes like this: After having seen an ad in the newspaper for a special on transmission repairs, we take our car to the garage complaining of a little transmission trouble. The mechanic then takes it apart. Now, the diagnosis may vary, but the price is usually about the same somewhere between 200 and 300 dollars. Well, after your cardiac arrest, you may decide you'd like to take your car to another shop for another opinion. The mechanic then informs you he's sorry, but he'll have to charge you at least 75 dollars or leave your transmission in pieces on the garage floor. At this point, you've been taken for at least 75 dollars. Should you decide to have it repaired at this shop—beware! The mechanic may make a needed adjustment, paint your transmission, and charge you about 300 dollars for a new one, or he can do something as simple as replacing a $20.00 vacuum modulator and charge you 225 dollars for a new rebuilt transmission. However done, it all adds up to a very profitable service.

Automotive transmissions may be the most popular area of deceitful practices, but unfortunately, they are not the only ones. Many frauds are worked when you simply leave your car at a service station

FIGURE 10.3   Continued

STUDENT ANALYSIS

STUDENT SPEECH

unattended, or step away to buy a soft drink. That's when the greedy operator has ample opportunity to pull one or more wires so the trouble lights go on or the car won't start.

Expert opinion

Specific examples

Changing Times, June 1974, tells of one technically minded bandit who was known to spray titanium tetrachloride, a colorless liquid that creates a dense white smoke, onto the alternator of cars. This successfully scared the wits and dollars out of many unsuspecting motorists. Another was known to pour common soda pop into the batteries of cars which made them foam profusely —another sale!

Transition

C. Incompetency:

Unfortunately, the questionable practices that many mechanics use to earn that extra buck are not at all uncommon. What I find more alarming is that many more mechanics are guilty of incompetency, and this incompetency is dangerous.

Statistics

Emotional appeal

Last year, for every 1,000 fatal accidents reviewed, 17 percent were the direct result of inadequate auto repair. Yet, daily, we deliver into these so-called technicians' hands, millions of incredibly complex machines in need of maintenance and repair.

Expert opinion

Statistics

Donald Randare, Washington based attorney and author of the book, The Great American Auto Repair Robbery, tells us that of the nation's 900 thousand auto mechanics, less than 40 percent have been classified as skilled labor by the Bureau of Census. The competency of the Auto Repair Industry leaves a great deal to be desired.

continued

FIGURE 10.3   Continued

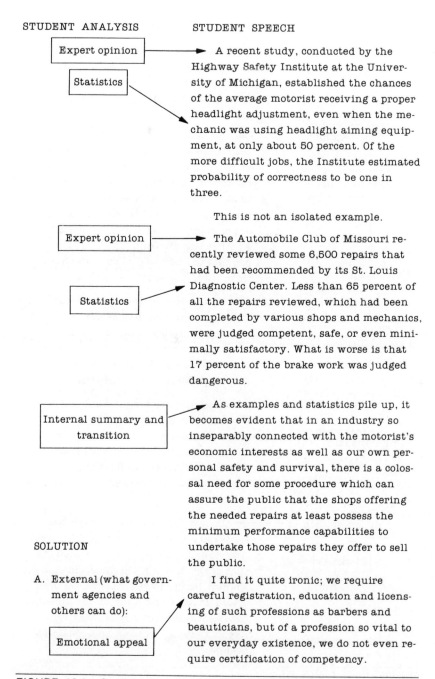

STUDENT ANALYSIS

Expert opinion

Statistics

Expert opinion

Statistics

Internal summary and transition

SOLUTION

A. External (what government agencies and others can do):

Emotional appeal

STUDENT SPEECH

A recent study, conducted by the Highway Safety Institute at the University of Michigan, established the chances of the average motorist receiving a proper headlight adjustment, even when the mechanic was using headlight aiming equipment, at only about 50 percent. Of the more difficult jobs, the Institute estimated probability of correctness to be one in three.

This is not an isolated example.

The Automobile Club of Missouri recently reviewed some 6,500 repairs that had been recommended by its St. Louis Diagnostic Center. Less than 65 percent of all the repairs reviewed, which had been completed by various shops and mechanics, were judged competent, safe, or even minimally satisfactory. What is worse is that 17 percent of the brake work was judged dangerous.

As examples and statistics pile up, it becomes evident that in an industry so inseparably connected with the motorist's economic interests as well as our own personal safety and survival, there is a colossal need for some procedure which can assure the public that the shops offering the needed repairs at least possess the minimum performance capabilities to undertake those repairs they offer to sell the public.

I find it quite ironic; we require careful registration, education and licensing of such professions as barbers and beauticians, but of a profession so vital to our everyday existence, we do not even require certification of competency.

FIGURE 10.3   Continued

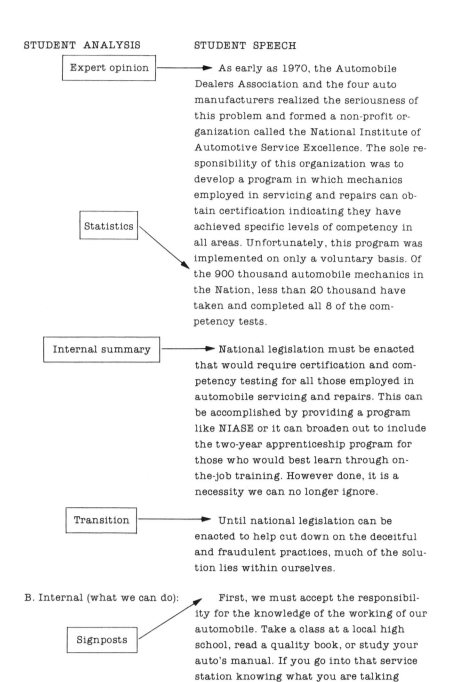

STUDENT ANALYSIS

STUDENT SPEECH

Expert opinion — As early as 1970, the Automobile Dealers Association and the four auto manufacturers realized the seriousness of this problem and formed a non-profit organization called the National Institute of Automotive Service Excellence. The sole responsibility of this organization was to develop a program in which mechanics employed in servicing and repairs can obtain certification indicating they have

Statistics achieved specific levels of competency in all areas. Unfortunately, this program was implemented on only a voluntary basis. Of the 900 thousand automobile mechanics in the Nation, less than 20 thousand have taken and completed all 8 of the competency tests.

Internal summary — National legislation must be enacted that would require certification and competency testing for all those employed in automobile servicing and repairs. This can be accomplished by providing a program like NIASE or it can broaden out to include the two-year apprenticeship program for those who would best learn through on-the-job training. However done, it is a necessity we can no longer ignore.

Transition — Until national legislation can be enacted to help cut down on the deceitful and fraudulent practices, much of the solution lies within ourselves.

B. Internal (what we can do): First, we must accept the responsibility for the knowledge of the working of our automobile. Take a class at a local high

Signposts school, read a quality book, or study your auto's manual. If you go into that service station knowing what you are talking

continued

FIGURE 10.3   Continued

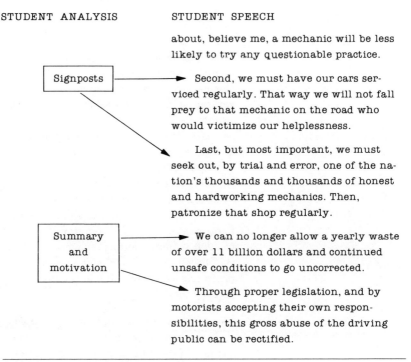

STUDENT ANALYSIS   STUDENT SPEECH

about, believe me, a mechanic will be less likely to try any questionable practice.

Signposts → Second, we must have our cars serviced regularly. That way we will not fall prey to that mechanic on the road who would victimize our helplessness.

Last, but most important, we must seek out, by trial and error, one of the nation's thousands and thousands of honest and hardworking mechanics. Then, patronize that shop regularly.

Summary and motivation → We can no longer allow a yearly waste of over 11 billion dollars and continued unsafe conditions to go uncorrected.

Through proper legislation, and by motorists accepting their own responsibilities, this gross abuse of the driving public can be rectified.

FIGURE 10.3   Continued

SUMMARY

This chapter has discussed the basic principles of public communication in business and organizational settings. A variety of business and community settings were listed, highlighting the most obvious audience settings for public communication, and the primary human interest reasons for business and industrial speeches were listed. Seven basic truths about the dynamics of public speaking were offered to explain why audiences continue to form for listening and why business continues to speak. A preparation guide for informative speeches was provided, and the elements of preparation were explained in detail. The general forms of the informative speech were discussed, and a set of guidelines for effective public speaking was provided.

Next, the persuasive speech was introduced, along with its

preparation guide. An example of a student speech was included, incorporating the various forms of proofs necessary to establish the speaker's claim for audience approval. Attention was also drawn to the speeches in Appendixes A through C for further study and example.

EXERCISES

1. Attend a local businesspersons' organization and take notes on the featured speaker. Talk with the speaker after the speech and learn as much as you can about his or her speech preparation and practice. Prepare a report for your class.
2. Take your best speech of the course so far and locate an audience outside of your class where you can deliver the talk. Learn as much as you can about the audience, talk with your instructor about the group, and, with your instructor's advice and your own analysis, adjust the speech to this new and "real" audience. Prepare a report for your class.
3. Interview a local business speaker of some renown about his or her theories and practices of public speaking. There is much to learn from a real public speaker who is constantly on the circuit. Prepare a report or discuss your assignment in class.

REFERENCES AND SUGGESTED READINGS

Kell, Carl L., and Winn, Larry James. 1976. *Guidebook in Public Communications*. Dubuque, Iowa: Kendall/Hunt. Pp. 85–90, 93–95.

Capps, Randall, and O'Connor, J. Regis. 1978. *Fundamentals of Effective Speech Communication*. Cambridge, Mass.: Winthrop. Pp. 159–164.

Chapter 11

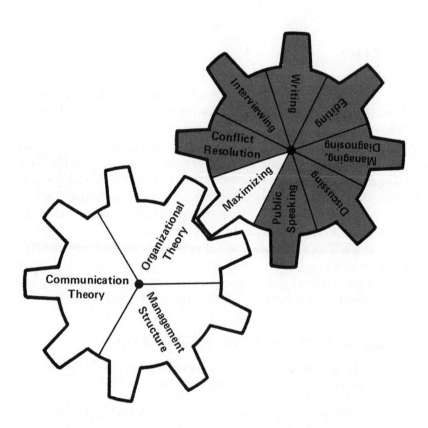

"I Forgot to Tell You"
MAXIMIZING COMMUNICATION SKILLS ON THE JOB

This chapter will provide you with the following:

1. the ability to list and discuss three ways to improve your listening skills on the job
2. the ability to identify and understand five common faults related to business communications and time management
3. the ability to identify and understand the four control guides for managing your time in the workplace
4. an understanding of the ten-item checklist of time management techniques
5. the ability to define the nature of stress
6. the ability to identify and understand basic stress reduction techniques
7. an understanding of the general nature of stress management for working women
8. the ability to identify and explain seven techniques for stress reduction in working women and men

Throughout the preceding chapters of *Let's Talk Business,* we have examined the general and specific areas of business communication that are directly related to optimum communicative effectiveness on the job. In this final chapter, our concerns will focus on the essentials of effective interpersonal communication as guidelines in determining when to use written or oral communication to maximize effectiveness and efficiency. The preceding ten chapters have meshed communication theory, organizational theory, and management structure with the skills of written and oral communication, and now we want to draw your attention directly to your role as a good listener, an effective time and stress manager, and a positive, assertive communicator in control of the communication environment. As a confident communicator, in command of your communication skills, you can perform your job as an efficient participant in phase I of your career (see Chapter 3).

IMPROVED LISTENING HABITS

Everyone likes a good listener, but not everyone likes to listen. Nearly one-third of our communication is oral, however, so we do not have much choice in the matter. Therefore, we must rethink our listening habits and determine how we can improve them. By understanding the factors that influence listening, some substantial improvement can be expected.

As a simple test, decide whether the following statements are true or false:

1. Listening is easy.
2. I can't listen if the speaker is boring.
3. Listening is just something you learn automatically.
4. Your ability to listen is basically related to how intelligent you are.
5. People who want to communicate with me have the responsibility to make me listen.

Did you answer any of these items as true? If you did, then this section on listening can help you develop a better appreciation of the subject.

Such elements in the communication environment as the clarity of the message, the importance of the message to the speaker and the listener, and the physical conditions under which listening takes place involve areas of potential problems. A good listener must eliminate as many possibilities for error as he or she can. The primary listening miscues are being too tired, bored, anxious, or uninterested in the subject matter. The following are several proper cues to improve your listening:

1. Determine your purpose in listening. Are you being sympathetic, receiving directions, listening for pleasure, gathering facts, or listening because you have to? Adjust yourself to take in the information, giving the speaker your full attention. This is more difficult when you are angry, anxious, or extremely unhappy. (Time and stress management are discussed later in this chapter.)

2. Learn how to listen to criticism. Job criticism from the boss, colleagues, or subordinates requires clear channels of reception not usually associated with distorted messages we think we are receiving. All criticism has a purpose, but it is often emotional and delivered in short oral bursts. Reserve judgment, fear, anger, and quick response as an automatic part of your communication style. Reflection on the criticism usually will produce a better response on your part. You can express real anger (if warranted), conciliation, compliance, or any other response once you have thought through the criticism. Listen, wait, think, plan your message, own your feelings about your message, deliver the message, and continue the dialogue started by the criticism. The end product will be a better understanding of the people you work with and may associate with for some time.

3. Take notes, in either abbreviated or outline form. You need to develop the habit of outlining extended communication experiences on the job, such as meetings, conferences, and interviews. Even if you have to reconstruct your thoughts,

note taking is a good idea. Notes of any kind help you arrange not only the messages you hear but the messages you send in short, face-to-face settings.

TIME MANAGEMENT

As you work now and prepare for your future career, the use of commonly accepted time management techniques can add hours to your day by providing some commonsense operating guidelines. Before taking good communication ideas and establishing them by written or oral means, we should examine five common faults related to business communication and time management.

1. *Moving too fast:* For the novice communicator, as for the novice jogger who runs two miles the first day of a running program, the second day often produces strains and pains. The temptation to cut back is strong, and, when less improvement results, the whole program may be stopped. Thus, a makeshift program of time management may be canceled before it is given a chance to work.

2. *Trying too much, too soon:* An employee fresh from business communication courses who tries to use several techniques at once, too soon, rarely understands that only one technique may be required. Too often, thought isn't given to beginning with one time-saving idea that can become a habit.

3. *Little attention to building time management habits:* Most employees fail to recognize that time management habits succeed only when they become a learned behavior pattern. Good time management habits don't happen over night. One technique is to take five to ten minutes of quiet time at least twice a day to think and plan. You can build the habit to blend with your normal daily activities. During these quiet times, you can arrange and prepare the combinations of written and oral messages that you need to send and the ones that you would like to receive.

4. *Little attention to resistance:* Any work place has a set pace or tempo of communication traditions and habits that have

been accepted as "the way things are done around here." Only a few new time-saving techniques stand any chance of acceptance. Resistance to new ideas about changing written or oral communication practices must be identified and ways to overcome such resistance must be developed. Communication sensitivity will tell you to expect small successes on the way to a future overhaul of traditional practices. Go slowly and expect frustrations from fellow workers. If you are right, time and your communicative common sense will overcome the obstacles.

5. *No decision on the most important beginning step:* Time management is a change program for your employer and a new workday process for the entry level employee. Change and new programs succeed in the same way, step by step. There must be small successes accomplished, so that failures along the way can be absorbed without severely damaging an entire program. Most important, the small successes must come fast on the heels of the first steps. Then, continuing to learn how to use time effectively will be easier as the other parts of the program are implemented.

STEPS TO SUCCESS IN TIME AND COMMUNICATION MANAGEMENT

As an employee, you must identify the factors in your day that can be controlled initially. Meetings, reports to be written, letters with deadlines, discussions, visitors, and phone calls—all these moments of communication can be harnessed as controllable elements in your day.

The first step is to identify specific communication events that eat into available work time. After this identification step, the measures to achieve communicative control can be specified more easily. Figure 11.1 provides a control guide that can be used for managing your time in the work place.

Of course, every successful attempt at handling time and communication demands meets with some failures. In order to meet

Factor	Extent of Control Possible	Steps to Achieve Control
1. Too many temptations	80%	Set up personal and job ground rules for visits. Get to the point of the communication demands and exit the encounter.
2. Lengthy phone calls	80%	Set up your series of calls in the morning and afternoon. (To be discussed later in this chapter.)
3. Drop-in visitors	90%	You can hold down time spent with surprise visitors by standing up throughout the session, lending a feeling of brevity to the chance meeting.
4. Emergencies	50%	Be brief and plan ahead so that you can leave the workplace or your location to attend to sudden changes in schedule.

FIGURE 11.1   Time management control guide

failure head on, you should ask yourself some basic questions about your own attitudes. Do you resist change in your personal life-style, for example, and if so, where and why? Why do you change your attitudes and under what specific circumstances do you experience change? Recall the last changes you made in your work setting and the reasons for those changes. As you answer these questions, you can identify the kinds of changes that you are most likely to adopt and predict the impact of changes on those with whom you work.

Generally, the time and communication techniques that work

best are those that are clear in their utility and small enough in scale so that their adoption—a new procedure in letter writing or an increase in sales meetings, for example—will not alter daily practice a great deal. Proposed changes in time management and communication procedures also should prove advantageous to your immediate superior and the work that occurs in your area of service. "We never did it that way before" is a common message in the business world. The reason this attitude hangs on is that the old ways often do prove more efficient. Saving time is not possible, but effective self-management and effective interpersonal communication can manage time.

Ask yourself how you would feel if someone told you to do something you didn't want to do. Before you develop small, new steps to improve your communication management and time management, you need to assess how you will react to your own ideas. You must be positive and assertive with the communication skills you learn from this text and from other sources, including your past and present job experiences. New ideas often are taken as threats and criticisms, so go slowly with others as you go easy with your advice to yourself.

To accomplish a fundamental change in your time and communication management, you need to concentrate on using time as effectively as possible, recognizing, of course, that time will always be moving on. Effectiveness means doing the right job at the right time, learning how to relax (stress management will be discussed later in this chapter), determining when *not* to work rather than trying to give the appearance of getting a great deal done, and using the clock to concentrate on priorities rather than on trivial chores. Don't become a perfectionist. Give each task the level of work it requires—no more, no less. With realistic standards, you can reduce the overall effort required to do all the necessary work.

How to be better organized

The following is a checklist of time management concepts that work for supervisors and managers and can work for you:

1. Know exactly what you are trying to do and what you want others to do. Minimize overlapping of work efforts. Are two people trying to do the same job?
2. Review job assignments regularly with employees. Be sure they understand their duties, roles, and so on.
3. Be sure that every employee knows to whom he reports and what issues he or she can and cannot decide (line of authority).
4. Delegate authority. Designate who is in charge so that a group leader is known by all concerned.
5. Employees are more effective and content if their duties are related. Assign related duties. In some instances, miscellany of duties is desirable, but this is the exception, not the rule.
6. Keep your organizational structure simple. People feel more comfortable and work best with things that are simple and understandable.
7. Evaluate employees' abilities. People's abilities improve or decline, jobs change, and new ideas develop. Look for change.
8. Make a "to do" list each day, listing A items (top priority), B items (work priorities), and C items (miscellaneous items, such as phone calls, visits, and so on). Arrange these areas of work so that each gets treated appropriately. As noted earlier, leave thinking time in your daily schedule so that A and B items can be dealt with fairly and on time. Remember—small accomplishments lead to habits of success.
9. Be organized. Reduce clutter and put things in order. You'll have more time, more space, and more efficient operation.
10. Divide and conquer. Procrastination—a real time killer —often results from tackling too big a job all at once. Dividing a problem can make it much more manageable.

In the world of work and business, time is money! Gain a sense of the value of time as money, and it will help make you more conscientious in developing and maintaining good time management habits.

Telephone communication

Most employees fear the telephone because it is seen as the most disruptive, uncontrollable force in an average work day. The following are some reliable, ethical ways to conclude a phone call and still obtain the information you need, while allowing the caller to exit the conversation gracefully:

- "I know you're busy, so I'll let you go."
- "Let me just say before we hang up . . ."
- "Listen, I'm going to have to let you go."
- "Can I call you back? I'm expecting a call."
- "Just let me make one last comment and then I really will let you go."
- "I've got to be in a meeting in two minutes."
- "Can we continue this conversation sometime later? Maybe lunch . . . ?"
- "Let me transfer you to . . ."
- "Can I have your number and . . ."
- "Someone is on the other line."

In order to plan a phone conversation so that you obtain the information you need, consider the following questions:

- Why am I calling?
- What kind of action do I want the receiver to take?
- Why should the receiver do what I suggest?
- What do I know about the receiver's personality that will help me persuade him to do what I want?
- If the receiver doesn't want to do exactly what I want him or her to do, what other actions or ideas can I suggest to accomplish at least part of my purpose?
- Can I overcome such factors as time of day, moodiness, and other situational elements and use them to my advantage?

Writing notes or drawing an outline often helps organize a telephone message before you place the call and also provides a record of the conversation. You might also keep a telephone log, as discussed in Chapter 8, to spot-check the amounts of time you spend telephoning and to show the order of calls made and received. A record of calls that spans days and weeks will help combine the information necessary for meaningful telephone communication. In short, *use* the phone; don't let it use you.

In summary, because all communication occurs within a time frame at the work place, your effective use of time on the job can lead to more efficient communication habits—the habits we have sought to share in the preceding chapters.

STRESS MANAGEMENT

Tied directly to management of your time and communication skills on the job is an ever-present problem—stress. In this hurried, active world, managing stress on the job is a never-ending battle for sanity, job effectiveness, and even job security.

As you enter the work force, you need to understand stress and how to manage the pressures of life on the job and even life at home. Maximizing your communication skills by budgeting your work and your time is one thing. Managing the sustained pressures you have to cope with daily is quite another thing.

The nature of stress

Stress is an automatic biological response to demands made on you, at work or at home. When these demands occur without warning, your body responds with a hormonal reaction known as fight-or-flight response, an adaptive response present in human beings since primitive times. The intensity and duration of the stress determines the amount of wear and tear on the body. The more often you experience the fight-or-flight response, the more vulnerable you become. The positive side of stress is that it can be appropriate, adaptive, and even life-saving. It enables us to work quickly under pressure, study late for an exam, get out of a touchy interpersonal problem, and meet our work deadlines.

In business, you are rarely in a position to give vent to your feelings. You have to control and hide your anger and overcome your fears. If there are insufficient avenues open for you to express your angers or fears, if you cannot find ways to reduce the stress impact on your central nervous system, your body suffers from being unable to discharge the intense, prolonged, and repeated tension. Paradoxically, a reduction in everyday work-related tasks because of illness, divorce, or vacation can also generate stress. What is even more surprising is that events that should be a cause of joy, such as a job promotion, can generate *new* stress because of new responsibilities.

In handling stress, steaming full speed ahead, fighting stress like a time perfectionist fights time, rarely works. A slower pace (not necessarily in time dimensions) activates less internal resistance and brings fewer antagonistic muscles into play. By focusing on the quality of performance on the job, you can tune down your stress in order to reduce the inhibitions that prevent maximum performance. You can also learn to regulate yourself to retain alertness while slowing your pace. Nonalertness and overactive stress response are the two extremes of stress management. Either form will cause you to overshoot the mark of effective job performance.

Stress management for the working woman

Stress is very different for the working woman than it is for the working man. We would be remiss if we did not give attention to a growing problem among the large female contingent in the work force. In today's work place, women have been led to believe that certain norms are expected for job success:

- You should try to be perfect.
- You should always work harder than anyone else.
- You should always answer every call.
- You should always worry about other people, or they will know you don't care about them.
- You should be able to have it all together—at home and at work.

The obvious results of these expectations are stress, anxiety, and depression.

The statistics in today's business world also reflect a stressful situation. Sources indicate that most women earn less than $200 a week, while most men earn more than $250 a week (Kinger, 1978). Only 3 percent of the women in the work force earn more than $500 a week, and only 6.5 percent of women are in management. The most stressful occupations for women are those that involve repetitive, boring, and dull work, with no chance of advancement. Among those in the most stressful jobs are secretaries, office managers, and laboratory technicians. Jobs that are personal and communicative in nature, such as personnel work, are more likely to be held by women, while jobs dealing with more impersonal concerns, such as budgets, are most likely to be held by men. It has been found that heart disease is more closely related to personnel-type jobs than to impersonal jobs. It is indeed unfortunate that jobs dealing with people, whether serviced by women or men, can lead to heart disease.

Living with stress

How do people learn to live with stress? We have some answers for entry job level employees facing the leveling nature of job stress.

There are many trade publications on the market that offer solid advice on business and life stress situations. We have listed some of the best books at the end of this chapter so that you can read more about the assets and liabilities of stress in our everyday lives. The following list is a summary of these suggestions for stress reduction:

1. With the fight-or-flight response possible at many moments in life and business, you should only fight for what is really worth the effort. You should not fly away from all other incidents, however, but exercise patience and careful interpersonal communication with others and with circumstances that cause a stress response.

2. When you experience defeat in your personal or business life, remember your past successes. The present moment won't feel so bad for too long.

3. "Don't put off what you can do now"—a modern version of the old adage of time management—is now a part of stress management advice. Stress and time are so interconnected in the fabric of our lives that, if we don't monitor our lives and our time, our interpersonal communication will be stifling and negative. If you are managing your work time, you will have time to either explode your stress in meaningful ways or tune down your stress when common sense dictates a milder response.

4. You must be positive about your work, choosing your responses to the work place with the human elements of trust and respect for your peers as your guides to business behavior.

5. Muscle relaxation therapy is an excellent way to reduce a basic muscular problem of stress. Although there are many suggested forms, a simple technique is as follows:
   - Sit in your favorite chair.
   - Close your eyes and relax all your muscles.
   - Breathe through your nose.
   - Rest in this position for ten to twenty minutes.

   This is simple, but it works.

6. All the literature on stress management argues strongly for vigorous exercise. The running craze of the past decade has gained momentum, as have a wide variety of participant sports. Ours is an active generation, and our careers have been and can continue to be better for it. Cardiovascular strength has become a watchword for millions of adults, and stress management has become a healthy by-product of our leisure lives. A regulated, active exercise program is a valuable asset in regulating the pressures of work. As human beings, we would all do well to blend our life and leisure with a steady diet of good food, rest, and exercise.

You might ask at this point what time and stress management have to do with optimizing interpersonal communication. We believe that these personal strategies for life undergird our self-concepts and thus our spirit to assert our communicative selves at work. If you can learn to arrange your time on the job more efficiently and handle your stress responses with appropriate actions, your communication practices will be carried out more easily. You can decide when to write a letter or memo that requires precision and when a personal conversation is necessary so long as your time is secure and yours to control and when you have decided on an effective message.

SUMMARY

In this chapter, we treated listening skills and time and stress management as the central issues in maximizing communication skills on the job. We identified five common faults related to business communication and time management. Next, we provided four control guides to assist you in managing your time in the work place. We then provided a nine-item checklist of time management techniques.

Closely associated with time use is stress management. We defined stress and identified and explained stress management for working women and men. Finally, we listed six techniques for stress reduction in working women and men.

EPILOGUE

We have come a long way since the first chapter's coverage of our national business and management structures. From what may have seemed an impersonal discussion of how business works to a deeply personal coverage of the basic communication skills required for entry job levels—phase I employees—*Let's Talk Business* has developed a theory and skills orientation for understanding communication in business. Throughout the text, we have been vitally concerned with telling you what to expect, how to prepare for the communication demands to be made on you, and how to strive for control of your business communication experiences.

There are no easy answers or magic formulas to make your mouth and hands work to perform amazing feats of communication. As the preceding chapters have indicated, the matters of everyday communication involve a set of skills to be acquired, fine-tuned, overhauled, and held constantly suspect. When we speak and write, we must be sensitive to the "other," the most important factor in the communication process. Whether to speak or remain silent and, if we speak, what to say and how to say it are all crucial decisions in the ordinary moments of our lives and our jobs.

Our hope for you is that your early days on the job and the future years of your career will be filled with exciting opportunities for success. We know that the vast majority of both personal and company failures in American business occur because of faulty communication skills. The message is simple and clear. Speak with clarity, write straightforwardly, and listen with care and concern. Become a total communicator so that you can say, with confidence, *Let's Talk Business!*

EXERCISES

1. In Chapter 8 we provided several communication logs to indicate how a business can monitor its communication practices. We have provided here a *personal* time log for you to monitor your weekly uses of time. Using the format here, set up a seven-day log with specific entries for each item. Be precise on every item. At the end of the time period, prepare a report analyzing your log and present your findings to the class.

PERSONAL TIME LOG

Job activities	Time spent
Commuting to and from work	
Meetings	
Telephone calls	
Reading, paperwork, and correspondence	
Aiding subordinates	
Drop-in visitors	
Seeing the boss	
Traveling on the job	
Calling on customers	
Miscellaneous job activities	

PERSONAL TIME LOG (continued)

Job activities	Time spent
Personal activities	
Grooming and personal care	
Eating	
Sleeping	

Family activities
Cooking
Laundering
Housecleaning
Yard work and household main-
   tenance
Shopping
Paying bills
Child care activities
Religious activities
Family outings
Family communication
Miscellaneous family activities

Leisure activities
Radio and music listening
Television viewing
Leisure reading
Hobbies
Spectator sports
Recreation
Parties
Miscellaneous activities

2. Attend a speech setting in which the communication factors or the speaker's faults make critical listening a difficult experience. Seat yourself as far away as possible and take notes about the situation. Compare your listening with that of a variety of people—those who sat closer, those who were required to attend, and those who attended because they wanted to. Prepare a brief summary report or devote part of a class period to sharing these common listener's experiences.

3. Conduct a series of information-gathering interviews with workers of all kinds in your community about their job stress and even life stress. Attempt to discover how your interviewees release their stress. Prepare a report or group discussion for your class. (Research on women in the work force might be an especially fascinating project.)

REFERENCES AND SUGGESTED READINGS

Mason, John L. 1980. *Guide to Stress Reduction.* Culver City, Calif.: Peace Press.

Kinger, Nora Scott. 1978. *Stress and the American Woman.* New York: Ballantine Books.

Selye, Hans. 1978. *The Stress of Life.* New York: McGraw-Hill.

Yates, Jere E. 1979. *Managing Stress—A Businessman's Guide,* New York: AMACOM.

Appendix A
A FEW WORDS ABOUT SPEECHES: RHETORIC IS ACTION

When I first went into business, my goal was to simply write speeches for other people and let it go at that. However, I found out rather quickly that many of my clients were not taking advantage of all the opportunities that giving a speech can generate ... such as press coverage and printed copies distributed to various people and publications. And so I began offering advice in these allied areas.

As a result, when I had my new brochures and business cards printed, I changed them from Confidential Speech Service to Charles A. Boyle, Writer/Consultant. But, I'm not as impressed by the term consultant as much anymore as I once was.

Lately, when I see the word consultant on a title or letterhead, I'm amused because it reminds me of the two old maids who live in my neighborhood. They have a big, black tomcat and they call him Sylvester.

It used to be that every night about ten o'clock, Sylvester would raise a fuss to get out of the house. And when they couldn't stand it anymore, the ladies would turn him loose to roam the neighborhood.

Of course, they wouldn't see him again until the next morning when he'd get hungry.

Speech delivered by Charles A. Boyle, writer/consultant, to the Mercer Island Rotary Club, Seattle, Washington, June 25, 1975, and published in *Vital Speeches of the Day* 41 (September 1975):682–685. Reprinted by permission.

Well, it bothered those two old maids to realize that Sylvester was having all that fun ... so they decided to do something about it and they took him down to the veterinarian where they had Sylvester fixed, figuring that would solve their problem.

The net result is that Sylvester still makes his evening calls ... but now he goes around as a consultant.

I stole that story from Mick Delaney ... a friend of mine who is a professional speaker. But I'm not a professional speaker ... I never get paid for giving a talk. I'm a professional writer and get paid for writing talks for other people to give. And everything I write is stolen from somebody. I want you to understand, however, that it's not plagiarism.

Plagiarism is when you take stuff from *one* writer ... when you take it from a lot of writers, it's called research.

In the course of my research for this talk I stumbled across some of the history of Johann Van Goethe.

I always thought of Goethe (if I ever thought of him at all) as simply the author of Faust and one of history's greatest writers.

But Goethe was more than a writer ... he was a politician and, in a friendly meaning of the word, a bureaucrat. Early in his career he held many civil offices and, with his extraordinary intelligence, was able to develop a keen understanding and deep insight of the people known as the general public.

Goethe believed ... and said ... "The public wishes itself to be managed like a woman: One must say nothing to it except what it likes to hear."

This could be done in Goethe's day, but if we use the popular ways of reaching the public in 1975 it's nearly impossible. To paraphrase Lincoln, we can tell some of the public what it wants to hear all of the time, but not all of the public what it wants to hear even some of the time.

The reason for this inability to please everybody with our words is that we try to reach the public simultaneously, instantly, and indiscriminately through the mass media. And since we are aware of the vast range of differing opinions in the radio, television, and newspaper audience, we begin thinking in defensive terms before we open our mouths rather than aggressive advocacy of our cause.

For we know that a large percentage of those listening will be in sharp disagreement with us ... no matter what we say.

Consequently, in an effort not to be too offensive to a large portion of that audience in a TV commercial, or when we speak in the presence of reporters, whenever we say black is black or white is white, we most likely qualify it by acknowledging every shade of gray.

Goethe didn't have this problem ... there was no mass media in his day.

When he spoke to the people of Frankfurt gathered in small audiences, he didn't have to dilute his remarks in fear of offending the people of Berlin or Munich. He knew the desires and needs of his audience in Frankfurt and spoke to them alone ... not to them and the people of Berlin at the same time.

A leading public relations counsel and author, Phillip Lesley of Chicago, put it this way ... "the more closely a communication is beamed to a specific audience, the more likely it is to be received and accepted ... each communication activity must reach SPECIFIC publics in ways that can gain THEIR interest and motivate THEIR support."

It's pretty hard to motivate the public while vacillating and apologizing.

But that's what's done too often by business and political leaders trying to tell their story through the mass media *alone*, because they KNOW they are not reaching a specific public ... they're hitting the whole spectrum of thought and opinion and pull their punches accordingly.

Whether deserved or not, business and government are under massive attack with no holds barred. And their defense, through the mass media, is soft-sell.

It's about all they can do in a 30 second radio or TV pop whether that 30 seconds is in the form of news or a commercial.

Lately, some industries began to realize that those 30 second announcements ... *alone* ... are not enough. More of the story has to be told and it takes longer than 30 seconds to do it.

Here's an example—

In the April 11, 1974 edition of the *Wall Street Journal*, the headline read ...

BIG OIL COMPANIES HIT LUNCHEON TRAIL TO BAT-
TLE BAD IMAGE

According to the journal story, many oil companies are
creating speakers bureaus or are expanding the ones they already
have.

A. D. Gill, who heads Gulf Oil Corporation's Vital Source
speakers bureau, says their program has been expanded from 200
speech-giving employees to 350. Gill says Gulf reached about 400
audiences in 1973 and one thousand audiences in 1974.

In the past year or so, the oil companies have probably been
the most visible targets of the "anti's." But the power companies,
lumber industry and phone companies are ships in the same con-
voy coming under attack. To some degree most of these industries
realize that a pretty ad alone cannot tell their story effectively and
gain support from the general public. And the general public, incidentally, really isn't totally committed to one side or the
other—but it does lack information from both sides of an issue.

As I mentioned, the oil companies . . . and some others . . . have
discovered that speaking to live audiences, where there is time to
say more than what can be said in a minute or less and where there
is an opportunity for face-to-face questions and answers, can be a
very effective way of getting a message across.

There is a rub, however. Too many speeches are done badly.

And, with typical American free enterprise initiative . . . or
what's left of it . . . a number of firms have cropped up recently to
teach the fundamentals of speech-making to company executives.

One of these firms is Carl Terzian Associates of Los Angeles.

Terzian personally receives two thousand requests a year to
give speeches and responds to about 200–250 of them.

Just to give you an example of how much money or trouble
some executives will pay for coaching, Terzian had one client . . . a
vice-president of a firm in Portland . . . who had Terzian meet him
once a month. Terzian would fly to Portland, meet his client at the
airport where they had lunch, coach him for an hour in a conference room, get back on a plane and return to Los Angeles.

Terzian told me . . . and it's been published in *California
Business* magazine . . . that on an average day in Los Angeles there
are 25 thousand audiences meeting. In New York, it's 40 thousand

a day ranging all the way from PTA's and high school assemblies to conventions, garden clubs and service clubs. And they all want a speaker.

When I first decided to go into my own business about 2 years ago, I wondered how many speeches were being given in the Seattle area. Using the Rotary Club as a barometer ... 20 clubs in the Seattle area meeting 52 weeks a year for about one thousand speeches at Rotary Clubs alone ... I figured that at least 5 or 6 thousand speeches were being given in Seattle each year. It's probably more like 1 or 2 thousand a day. Or more.

The audiences are there and always have been.

Speeches are a great way to reach the public ... and the best way to reach and tell a story to specific publics.

But only if the speeches are done effectively.

The trouble is, too many speeches are deadly.

How many times have you heard the phrase ... "I have to go and listen to a speech?"

What a negative reaction to speeches that is!

And yet, almost every great thought of mankind was first expressed in a speech.

Aristotle, Socrates, and Cicero gave speeches that were taken down in shorthand by slaves and then written in longhand and—in the case of Cicero—sold to the public.

Shakespeare wrote plays which were mostly speeches.

Or even today, how many people can remember the words John Kennedy wrote in his book, *Profiles in Courage?*

How many people can forget what he said in his inauguration speech ... "Ask not what your country can do for you, but what you can do for your country."

Which, incidentally was first said in a speech about 300 years ago by Frederick the Great of Prussia.

I ask you ... can you quote from the books of Winston Churchill? Can you forget his phrase ... "the iron curtain" ... given in a speech at Columbia, Missouri?

Newton Minow may be a name the public cannot remember. But the public remembers what he called television in a speech ... a vast wasteland.

From Washington's farewell to Lincoln's Gettysburg Address... to Roosevelt's "We have nothing to fear" to Churchill's blood, sweat and tears, the list of memorable speeches is endless.

Good speeches are *printed* and *quoted* and *remembered*.

The audiences can be far greater than those present at the time they are given.

But none of those great speeches was given spontaneously.

None of those great men got up before an audience, hemming and hawing, stumbling and searching for words... trying to put thoughts into continuity at the same time they were speaking.

They put their thoughts in order on paper BEFORE they spoke.

Whether you agree with their words or not, good speakers... while on the platform... never give you the uncomfortable feeling that you have to help them out. You won't see them groping around for words while you squirm and say to yourself... "come on, I know the word you're looking for... say it."

Mark Twain said... "it usually takes more than three weeks to prepare a *good, impromptu* speech."

But the sin of most people called on to give a speech is that they direct their efforts in proportion to the size of the audience.

For instance, if a businessman was given the opportunity to speak to the 500-member downtown Rotary Club, he would probably be willing to pay a fee for help in coming up with a good speech.

But if that same businessman was asked to speak to a small Rotary Club in some suburb, he might not be too anxious to go to any expense over it.

Yet, with one good speech he could give it to 15 small Rotary Clubs, not only reaching a bigger audience than the downtown club, but some of the people doing make-ups at the smaller clubs.

I had one client last year who gave the same speech 30 times to 30 different groups in a period of one month. He was giving that speech every day or evening... sometimes twice a day. He not only reached two thousand people in person, but parts of his speech were quoted in the two big daily papers the first time he gave it and in the neighborhood weeklies the rest of the month.

I'm happy to say he was promoting a certain cause and it was successful.

Giving a speech is sort of like being on the stage. I suppose there's a little bit of the ham in all of us and, if we perform well, favorable attention will be directed our way.

I'm sure you've all heard of movie actors who want to be in Broadway plays . . . they want to see and feel the reaction of the audience.

Even Lloyd Cooney, who's on television every day, still likes to give speeches where he can be in touch with his audience.

And he always reads his speeches.

But speakers and potential speakers are told time and time again that they should never . . . never, use a script or read a speech.

That's ridiculous . . . unless you happen to be a professional speaker. And you'd be amazed at how many professional speakers use scripts . . . it just looks like they aren't.

When's the last time you ever saw a president or a governor give a speech without a script? And it if was on television and they didn't have a script in front of them . . . you can bet it was on the teleprompter.

Even Lincoln wrote the Gettysburg Address . . . not once, but five times. Parts of it were used in other speeches for years before he spoke those immortal words in Pennsylvania. And when he gave it, he had the script in his hand, in spite of the fact that it was only about two minutes long.

Businessmen and political leaders should always use a script. After all, once they utter the words . . . they can't be erased. And by talking from the top of your head, even if you've mentally outlined your talk or are using notes, the wrong words have a way of slipping out inadvertently and the right word is too often forgotten at the moment. This can't happen if a script is followed faithfully.

The trouble with most speech writers, however, is that they write material that's great to read at your leisure. But someone has to stand up and SPEAK that speech. The good speech writer knows that and writes for an oral presentation . . . for the EAR.

There's a great deal of difference between material that is written to be read and material written to be heard.

Another, anti-script argument is that some people think it's an insult to an audience to read a speech. I think it's a compliment . . . by putting your thoughts down in the form of a script, you are, in effect, saying that you care enough for your audience's time to spend hours ... not talking and rambling ... but researching and writing. And people who are experts in their field usually have enough knowledge and information about their field to talk for hours. The trick is to boil it down to the time frame allotted and still make the essential points.

As for the person who hires a professional to put his knowledge into a concise presentation; if the audience should guess or know that someone else wrote the speech, the person that hired the writer is telling the audience that he cares enough about them to spend some money to give them the best talk he can.

One of the things I always try to do myself, and depending on the type of audience, advise my clients to do, is never to go to the bitter end of the allotted time with a prepared talk, but leave some time for questions and answers. That's what I'm about to do now. But I can't resist slipping in at least one bit of philosophy which may be appropriate to our times.

In recent years the word rhetoric has been demeaned. Perhaps you've heard people say, in effect, no more rhetoric ... let's have some action.

Well—rhetoric *is* action. Plato said, "Rhetoric is the art of ruling men's minds." And, of course, once you've ruled their minds, you rule all of them. I think it's time businessmen ... who are men of action ... start sharpening their skills of rhetoric. Lord knows, the people tearing down business have been using it.

I think businessmen should be blowing their own horn more often, for—as W. S. Gilbert put it—"If you wish in the world to advance—your merits you're bound to enhance; you must stir it and stump it, and blow your own trumpet, or trust me, you haven't a chance."

Appendix B
IS YOUR PRODUCT READY FOR THE MARKET?

Good morning:

When a "local" is asked to speak to a group like this on an occasion as important as this, it's tempting to ask oneself, "How come—couldn't they get someone else, did the one selected get sick at the last moment, or do they really want to hear what I think about things?" Irrespective of why I was asked, I am delighted to have the opportunity, and I feel highly honored to be a part of this Teacher Appreciation Breakfast.

Hopefully, I may make some small contribution to it.

Some time ago Tom Cisar called my attention to an article with approximately the same title I've given to these remarks. I enjoyed reading it because it talked at length about the necessary inter-relation, or inter-action, if you will, of schools and industry. And the more I thought about it, the more I thought that the topic was timely, although recognizing that the main thrust of the article was not necessarily what I wanted to say.

While I started my adult career as a teacher—believe it or not teaching astronomy at the University of Michigan—it didn't last long. The family business called, and after a reasonable period of indoctrination I became a salesman. Believe me, when I was doing

Speech delivered by Cass S. Hough, President, Recreation Products group, Daisy Heddon Division, Victor Comptometer Corporation, Rogers, Arkansas, to the Rogers Chamber of Commerce Teacher Appreciation breakfast, August 24, 1971. Printed by permission of the author.

my four years of undergraduate work and one year of graduate work, becoming a salesman was farthest from my mind. But all of a sudden, there I was, so to speak, with a sample case in each hand, a small expense check and a rather hazy knowledge of how to go about producing the results I was *expected* to produce.

Since that time most of my activity has been in products of one sort or another and their related activities. And it is from this viewpoint I am going to visit with you for a little while this morning.

In my forty-five years at Daisy, as a member of the Toy Manufacturers of America and for two years its president—as a student of industry and its practices—I've watched a lot of products come and go. I've seen more products fail in the market place—more *by far*—than I saw succeed. Almost without exception, the failures have been the direct result of the product not being ready for the market, (although I must admit, occasionally, the shoe has been on the other foot and the market has not been ready for the product). This "unreadiness" takes many forms or combinations thereof, but the result is the same—*no sale!*

It's my opinion that the development of a successful product through all its stages has a direct correlation with what you are doing. History proves that the doing of the job properly produces a salable product, and conversely, failure to do things properly results in product failure.

What, then, in outline form, without all the "nitty gritty" is the process which eventually produces a product; and, more importantly, what are the processes that almost guarantee a reasonable degree of success. And, also, what are some of the things that almost guarantee the failure of products in the market place.

In my opinion, there are really only two basic types of products. The kind that people need, such as clothing, food and shelter (and today, I suppose, a form of transportation); and the products that could be looked upon as icing on the cake—desirable, interesting, entertaining, but not vital. But, regardless of the type of product, whether it is vital or desirable, if it is to be marketed, the first step in doing it is to secure an indepth knowledge of the market. Answers to the following—Is it needed? Who needs it? Why do they need it? How many need it? How badly do they need it? Can it be made and sold at an attractive price? or, if it is not *vitally* needed, can a need, or perhaps more rightly, a desire, be created? And if so, how? Regardless of the *degree* of need, a full and complete knowledge of the market for a product must be had, if the marketing is to be successful. In my opinion, this holds just as true for your product, a graduate, as it does for an item of consumer goods.

Do you know, in depth, the market for *your* product? Let's assume then that a critical indepth study has been made of the market—that the need has been established, the degree of need has been established. That the product will remain sold, because its quality and performance is all that is expected. And because time really doesn't permit an examination of each facet of this kind of study, we'll make the assumption that we have a viable product and we've decided to make it.

The engineering has been done, the specifications are laid out, tooling is in process. Advertising is studying various types of appeals. Sales Promotion is studying the various methods of promoting the item to the Trade itself. Personnel and Production have together looked at the people requirements, the impact on the machinery, Finance has studied the cash requirements, how much and when it is going to be required, as compared to what's available—all these things have been done—everything is pointing to the day, maybe even the hour when the new product is ready to ship. How often do you test your product against all these criteria?

If the homework has been done properly and evaluated properly, no one really needs to hold his breath to see if it will sell—there remains only the degree of saleability. And on paper at least this degree of saleability is not seriously in doubt. However, if anywhere along the line, any one of the criteria used in arriving at the final decision, has not been updated—if anyone charged with the major responsibility for measuring the probable success or failure has leaned on *old* information, this product may fall far short of its anticipated potential; its acceptability as a new item in the market may be handicapped seriously by the failure of some one or ones to keep abreast of the market. And I would remind you that very often during the many many months lead time between product conception and production, in your case, say, in the last two years of school, major changes occur in the market place. This is another way of saying that just because all the lights were green, say fifteen months ago, doesn't mean that *any* of them are green at the time the product is ready for the market. What I am trying to say is that there is no maintaining the status quo—*not for one single minute.*

Now it's reasonable for you to say "We accept your analysis of the marketing problem and the steps necessary to solve it successfully—but how does that concern us?" Your end product, a high school graduate, must be the product of teaching methods resulting from an indepth continuous study of the market place. These methods must be constantly scrutinized for their validity in *today's* market. You recognize this I am sure—you go to school in the summer time, many of you do, you read available material on this business of education, you go to Seminars—all to update yourself in *teaching methods.* But what do you do to be reasonably sure that these methods will produce an *end product* that is readily saleable to today's market? Keeping updated in *teaching methods only* is very much like a business that constantly updates *only* its machinery. But if that's all that a business does, before long, it won't need that machinery. This is, perhaps, another way of asking you if you know or attempt to find out what the average business looks for in a prospective employee *today.* In other words, is your product ready for today's market.

Briefly let me tell you our views of today's market in *this* frame of reference.

As a Company we pursue excellence. No one talks about this much, perhaps because it seems so obvious; but maybe the pursuit of excellence is not so obvious. Judged by the trouble they go to achieve it, or by their willingness to pay for it, certainly most of our customers, suppliers or competitors, seem to recognize its importance. *We* only hear about excellence when our products don't perform up to snuff.

We all want excellence in what *we pay* for, but quite often we are unwilling to provide it in what *we get paid for.* When it comes to selling a product, yours or ours, the passing grade is one hundred percent, not sixty-five percent. We can't sell a product that performs only sixty-five percent of the time, *nor can you.*

And this is a fact that must be driven home to your students. Time and *time again* it must be driven home. It's what any company must provide if it is to remain in business; and it's what you must provide if this gigantic business of education is to survive, and improve, to meet the challenges of today.

In my opinion the underlying thrust of the educational system must be to motivate the individual towards achieving real *quality* in *himself. If* he is *so* motivated he will realize that the passing grade is *not* sixty-five percent. *It must be one hundred percent.* I would remind you (and you must constantly remind people who come in contact with you) that, after all, it's only people of excellence who build greatly and lastingly. Remember that Egypt had millions of people living on the world's most fertile soil, whereas Athens had only some two hundred thousand people living on a rocky plain. What do we remember of Egypt of old?—Cleopatra! While Athens to us symbolizes great architectural monuments, nobility of thought, and the birthplace of the democratic institutions. So Athens is imperishable, and Egypt—well, it's there!

Excellence is a *thing in itself,* and certainly can't be limited to any one particular kind of activity or measured by any common standards. Certainly there is excellence in abstract intellectual activity, in art, in music, in managerial capacities, in craftsmanship, and ability to work at the work bench.

There are sound standards of craftsmanship in every calling and these standards have to be met by the people in these callings. Every honest calling, and every walk of life has its own elite, its own aristocracy, based upon excellence of *performance.* The person of *quality* will take *delight* in craftsmanship, whether he is building a bird house, writing a novel, supervising a Production Department, or simply running a machine. He is impelled *by his principles* to do well *habitually,* what it is his job to do.

And I honestly believe that to seek quality in one's work, one must have a substantial motive. It's my opinion that the anguish of an empty life—one without objective *or* motivation—far more than any economic condition or political injustice—is the thing that drives people to demonstrate and demand, instead of studying and earning. (REPEAT FROM "IT'S MY OPINION")

Captain James Cook, one of the early explorers, said, "I had ambition not only to go farther than any man had ever been before, but as far as it was *possible* for a man to go."

People of excellence down through the years have sought and found problems to be solved. They recognize that it isn't enough to be against error and ignorance, because *that* leaves the impression that error and ignorance are the *active* forces in the world, and that we are just a formless mass opposing them. Instead of denouncing or denying what others bring forth as the truth, great men offer their own truths.

A product must possess excellence if it is to sell and stay sold and excellence in the market is not just a passing grade of sixty-five percent. And excellence is not the willingness on the part of an *employee* to just do a job well—he must be imbued with the desire to do even better.

If you think I am hipped on the subject of excellence, so be it, because I am.

Many are blessed with capabilities, but performance is a *transformation* of these capabilities by application and work. One of the earliest Greek poets said, "The high gods have erected a formidable barrier of sweat before the Gates of Excellence."

So then, in getting your product ready for the market you have the responsibility for, and are probably the only ones who can, imbue in these youngsters a *desire for excellence.* You must help them appreciate the need for personal devotion to the idea of excellence, to help them avoid what, in my opinion, is the saddest state for an intelligent being—the state of regretting what *might* have been, when it's too late to take another path.

And finally, in helping others strive for excellence, you must practice, continuously, self-renewal.

We are all aware of the present-day information explosion, new textbooks, curricula revisions, and supplementary materials that are prepared almost faster than you can absorb them. I'm sure you often feel that you are simply a data transmitter in your efforts to advance your students.

But unfortunately simply to transmit information is not enough. Students, to keep up with the world into which they will graduate, must learn in school how to *keep learning through life,* how to use information effectively, how to keep on top of changes that are inundating the unprepared. And this is the continual striving for excellence. Not just in school, but continuously.

The present situation in the classroom may be likened to that of a teacher attempting to teach his students all the words in the dictionary. But this is an Alice in Wonderland kind of dictionary because the terms change as you look at them and so do their definitions. Because this condition exists, you must realize that self-renewal must be a continuing job for all of us. If we don't practice it, we certainly can't expect to *teach* this continuing self-renewal to the people who look to us for guidance. And if we *don't* teach it, then our product is not ready for the market—and it won't SELL!

Appendix C
THE SPEAKER AND THE GHOST: THE SPEAKER IS THE SPEECH

First of all, I must confess that I'd like to ask all of the speechwriters in the audience to get up and leave. The number one rule of speechmaking is this: Never speak to your professional peers! It scares you to death! That's why economists are in such demand as speakers. No one understands economics, so economists feel very comfortable talking to everyone. They even feel comfortable talking to each other because they all disagree.

Actually, we are all speechmakers—and we all practice our speeches in our imaginations before we actually deliver them to our husbands, wives and children. My mother was the first speechmaker that I really noticed. Did you ever notice how mothers deliver speeches to their children? I think that they all secretly long for a podium. My mother's first speech was the one about my face. (Mothers have a way of getting personal in their speeches right away.) She would say, "Look at that expression on your face. Do you want your face to freeze into that expression? Go look in the mirror—you're about to step on your lip." Then came the speech about how faces are a reflection of the person's spirit. I'm sure your mothers had speeches, too. And those

Speech delivered by Carolyn Lomax-Cooke, Communications Specialist, Cities Service Company, to the Tulsa Chapter of the International Association of Business Communicators, Tulsa, Oklahoma, October 20, 1981, and published in *Vital Speeches of the Day*, December 1, 1981. Reprinted by permission.

speeches were delivered with such frequency and conviction that you remember them.

But how many other speeches do you remember? How many other speeches would you actually consider "good"?

Tonight I want to talk candidly about what makes a good speech, a good speaker and a good speechwriter. Please notice that I am emphasizing "good" in each instance. We have all heard unimpressive speeches. But what we want to look at tonight is that special quality that makes a speech memorable.

My message is very simple—for the good speech, the good speaker and the good speechwriter all center around one understanding of the speech occasion. And that understanding is this: the speaker IS the speech. The man IS the message. The woman IS her words. If the speaker and the speechwriter understand this fundamental of a good speech, all will go well. If the partners fail at this point, so will the speech.

But what do I mean—the speaker IS the speech? I mean that the listener cannot separate the content of the message from the character of the speaker. During a speech, the message itself and the vehicle through which it is delivered (the speaker) are so integrated that when the audience evaluates one, it automatically evaluates the other. The speaker and the speech are one and the same.

Communications professors get fancy about theory at this point. They say that speeches appeal on three levels. One level is source credibility, called "ethos." Another is the emotional appeal of the speech, called "pathos." Third is the so-called "logos" level, which relates to the rational, factual appeal of the speech. But when you subtract the Greek from this theory, you will find that professors are saying some very simple things about the human nature involved in listening to a speech. The listener asks three questions as he listens to a speechmaker. He asks: "Is this speaker reliable? Do I like him? Can I trust his facts?" And whether the speaker likes it or not, these questions will be answered through his own personality and character as he delivers the speech—not through statistics, charts, or intricate explanations of technical data.

Since the audience responds to personality and character, the good speaker will take care that the speech truly reveals his character. Personality, life, conviction, excitement or despair—these must shine through the speech as a reflection of the speaker. The audience recognizes such honesty and always responds to personal stories, ancedotes about the speaker's family, or a reference to a book that the speaker has read. Because let's face it, the audience came to hear the speaker—not to watch a human body mouth the words of a written treatise.

When Hannah introduced me, she said that I have written more than 40 speeches during the past three years. What she didn't tell you is that many of those speeches are unimpressive, simply because they fail at this point of integrating the speech and the speaker.

And I can tell you right now that if you are interested in being a speechwriter, you will face this same difficulty. Many corporate speechmakers simply do not want to reveal any hints about themselves as people. They want to strike all references to their outside activities, to their opinions, to their personal experiences. They honestly believe that the audiences want facts—not warm human beings. Also, these guys are just plain modest. They don't want to draw any attention to themselves. And, like all other speakers, they are nervous. I read in the *Wall Street Journal* that Maurice Granville, former chairman of Texaco, complained to his wife about his nervousness when speaking. Her advice for him was wonderful. She said: Look out there and just imagine all those people in their underwear, and that will make you feel better about it. Granville reports he tried it and it worked. But mostly executives just want to deliver the facts and get off the stage.

What is the result of these corporate speeches? When the speaker is not the speech—when the content of the speech does not reflect the character of the speaker—the audience responds with the same emptiness which the speaker delivered. Mistrust and lack of persuasion result.

Just look at oil industry speaking activities. The American Petroleum Institute has calculated that during 1980 more than 4,000 oil industry speakers addressed more than 18,500 different audiences. If those audiences held an average of 50 people, then oil industry spokesmen talked to almost 1 million people in 1980 alone! And oil industry people have had active speaking programs for years.

Yet what are the results of this activity? Studies show that almost 80 percent of the general American public still believe that oil industry profits are out of line. Only 13 percent of the public is "very confident" of the industry. And half of the public still thinks that the oil industry should be broken up into separate producing, transportation, refining and retail companies.

Somewhere along the line, oil industry speakers have failed to impress their audiences with their thinking—and I am willing to bet that they have failed because they did not recognize the one fundamental which I have stressed: that the man IS his message, and that his personality must shine through the content of his speech in order for him to be believable.

Conversely, every truly impressive speech that you can remember is memorable because of the melding of speech content with the speaker's character and life experiences.

For instance, no one but Aleksandr Solzhenitsyn could have delivered his stirring Harvard commencement address in 1978. No one but this great Russian author—rejected by officials of his nation, imprisoned for his writing and finally exiled from his country—could speak so convincingly about the important things in life such as honor, courage, strength and conviction about eternal things. Who but Solzhenitsyn could say this to Harvard graduates, "I could not recommend your society as an ideal for the transformation of ours. Through deep suffering, people in our country have now achieved a spiritual development of such intensity that the Western system in its present state of spiritual exhaustion does not look attractive." Only he could say this—out of his own experience.

And who but Barbara Jordan could have delivered her powerful keynote address at the 1976 Democratic Convention? This black Congresswoman, with her forceful voice, said: "A lot of years have passed since 1832 (when the first Democratic Convention met to nominate a Presidential candidate), and during that time it would have been most unusual for any national political party to ask that a Barbara Jordan deliver a keynote address . . .

but tonight here I am, and I feel that notwithstanding the past that my presence here is one additional bit of evidence that the American Dream need not forever be deferred."

From that point on, the audience was hers. She was the speech and the message was hers alone. No one else could have delivered it. . . .

You can see through these examples that when the speech is good, it is because the speaker is the speech, the woman is her words. But if the speech must reveal the speaker in a personal way in order to be effective—what is the role of the speechwriter?

I said earlier that the speaker and the speechwriter are partners. They are, but the ghost writer is the silent partner. A behind-the-scenes person. In fact, almost an invisible person.

The speechwriter is a server—one who serves the speaker in a variety of ways. Foremost, the speechwriter must keep in mind the fundamental which I have harped on for the past ten minutes—that the speech and the speaker are one. The ghost writer must make the message come alive through anecdotes, testimonies, humor from the speaker's point of view. The executive will likely resist efforts to personalize his or her comments. Your job as a speechwriter is to encourage him and persuade him that the audience asked to hear his ideas—not yours.

Then—and only then—should the writer focus on the practical aspects of speechwriting. The speechwriter's first service is to do extensive research. You must become an expert in the speaker's fields of interest. It is your job to keep up with daily developments in those areas. This involves a lot of newspaper and journal reading.

Secondly, the speechwriter serves by writing with the flair and polish that the corporate speaker generally lacks. You must learn to write for the ear, not the eye. You are not a novelist, not a journalist, not an editor of a company newspaper. You are a speechwriter—and speeches require a different cadence, a different vigor than do editorials and news articles. You can learn this skill by reading other good speeches, by writing a lot of bad speeches and getting embarrassed when they fail, and by delivering speeches yourself to see what works.

And now, I want to give you some tips about how to actually

create the speech. Write this first tip indelibly upon your hearts and minds—no matter what your boss says, call the speaker before researching or writing one word of a speech. Even if you have to do it on the sly (and many of us have done it that way), call the speaker and ask him what he wants to say to this particular audience. Set up a meeting with him so that you can establish a rapport with him, and so that you can help him develop his ideas. I must warn you that he may not have any ideas. It happens—frequently.

Then it is your job to do as much research as time allows. Check newspapers, books, polling services, professional organizations, interview experts in the field—any source which might have material that involves the subject of the speech. Read the material as time allows. Don't spend a lot of time taking notes, because when you actually write the speech your message must be painstakingly simple.

Next, write your outline. You should be able to summarize a good speech in one or two sentences. Then develop that main idea all you want. Use illustrations, quotes, facts to amplify the idea. But do not have five main points and ten subpoints which you want to make. Your audience will never remember past point number one. And your speaker will get lost in the intricacy of his message.

This actually happened to a corporate executive recently. He was speaking to a large group—using a very impersonal, well-written speech with complicated information and lots of slides. When he was through, a woman stood up and asked him what his purpose was in talking to her group. He couldn't answer the question. He couldn't remember why he was there! He even tried to turn the question over to the moderator. He lost all credibility through that exchange.

You've summarized your main points and outlined the speech. Now is the time to put ink on paper. To exercise the creative power of words. This is the time to use all the flair and skill you have as a writer. This is the time to use those personal tidbits you have collected which reveal the speaker. Don't let yourself lapse into that special lingo called "corporate English." We laugh at our office about the guys in the Company who write that they have "jumboized" their tankers. Others are in the process of "prioritizing in-puts." I implore you to say what you mean in straightforward English. Audiences shouldn't be called upon to translate speeches as they listen to them.

Many writers worry about length of the speech. Most speeches run about 20 minutes, but audiences have been mesmerized for more than an hour by speakers who really have a message for them—so worry about the message, not length when you are writing the speech.

Finally, you must face the approval process. Here a new series of difficulties begin—internal politics. Send the speech to the speaker and your bosses AT THE SAME TIME. A good speech cannot survive a long approval line. All corrections (except for fac-tual changes) should be made directly between yourself and the speaker. Otherwise, all liveliness and honesty will evaporate from your words.

Does this process sound time-consuming? It is. A reporter once asked Truman Capote why he could not produce a book in two weeks, as another writer claimed he could. Capote retorted: "That's not writing, that's typing!"

Speechwriting takes time, too—it's not a matter of "just typ-ing." The final product is the speechwriter's reward: A speech oc-casion where the speaker is the speech and the audience responds warmly to the life of the message.

Finally, a word of encouragement. If you do not think you can tolerate ghost writing speeches—become a mother or father in-stead. Then you can practice and deliver your own speeches to a captive audience! And if you are fortunate, you may even see some good results coming from your performances!

Appendix D
COMMUNICATION COMPETENCES: RANK ORDER OF IMPORTANCE IN SKILL AREAS

Human relations

Display integrity and honesty in all communications.
Recognize the limitations of your own inquiry system and that of others.
Understand and compensate for your own and others' biases.
Analyze motivating factors of yourself and others in interpersonal interactions.
Form a valid image of others.
Understand the determinants of morale.
Recognize that the nature of the relationship between persons is a product of the interaction between them rather than of the traits or behavior of any person individually.

Interviewing

Conduct information-seeking interviews.
Demonstrate versatility in the use of questions.

Listening and feedback

Solicit feedback from those with whom you communicate.
Provide feedback to those with whom you communicate.
Listen empathetically.
Restate statements made by others to reflect their meaning accurately.

Message

Understand that we never have complete control over how our messages may be interpreted.

Recognize that meaning is in people.

Understand the role of perception in the interpretation of information.

Organize facts and data in easily understood, meaningful patterns.

Write clear, concise, objective messages.

Avoid relying on single information sources.

Distinguish between various types of statements (factual, inferences).

Identify concepts and supporting arguments of others.

Avoid semantic breakdowns of communication.

Tolerate considerable ambiguity in responses to messages.

Organizational functions

Communicate laterally within an organization.

Communicate downward within an organization.

Communicate upward within an organization.

Understand the role structure of organizations and how role expectations influence communication behavior.

Communicate to the right people within the organization.

Anticipate the communication needs of those with whom you work.

Evaluate the impact of your personal communication habits and patterns on the organization.

Understand the concepts of communication networks and recognize potential problem areas.

Personnel relationships

Recognize the tendency of subordinates not to express negative reactions or problems.

Review the performances of subordinates without creating defensive reactions.

Handle touchy situations tactfully.

Understand the language patterns and needs of minority groups and women in the organization.

Demonstrate skill in giving and testing employee or subordinate understanding of instructions.

Power and conflict

Deal constructively with conflict situations that arise within the organization.

Recognize the effects of power and status differences on communication behaviors.

Negotiate effectively with other organizational units.

Small groups

Recognize the task-oriented and social needs of groups.

Discriminate among various managerial and leadership styles.

Effectively apply small group research findings to small groups within organizational settings.

Theory

Understand the differences between one-way and interactive interpersonal communication.

Understand the behavioral process of communication.

Appendix E
OUTLINING

Careful outlining is the first step toward a successful talk. Outlining means simply to place in order according to a system.

I. Outlining saves the speaker.
   A. A finished outline shows the speaker the succession of ideas he or she will give.
   B. An outline assures that the speaker has chosen and arranged to the best of his or her ability the material that will help realize his or her purpose.
   C. By looking at the finished outline, the speaker will be able to see if he or she has omitted any main points or any minor points needed for support.
   D. An outline answers the questions: "What shall I say?" and "In what order shall I say it?"
II. Outlining saves time.
   A. It assures brevity in speaking and conservation of time.
      1. An outline helps you deliver your speech without hesitations and without rambling.
      2. Brevity and clarity are pleasing to the listener.
      3. By pleasing the listener, you are supporting your cause.
   B. The outline of the talk is like the architect's plan of the building, the dressmaker's pattern, the engineer's drawing of the bridge.

  1. These people have definite aims in mind and they must
     achieve their goals by choosing the most efficient
     method.
  2. Each of them visualized the completed project before
     beginning construction, just as the speaker does in
     preparing an outline.
  C. Outlining helps maintain a certain balance or proportion.
     1. The effective speaker introduces his or her main points
        quickly.
     2. He or she then supports the main points logically.
     3. Then he or she concludes or summarizes.
III. Outlines require a lettering system.
  A. The I-A system is most common.
     1. Figures alternate with letters throughout the outline.
        I.
           A.
              1.
                 a.
                    (1)
                       (a)
     2. This system of outlining meets the requirements for a
        speech outline by being easy and logical.
     3. All capital letters (A, B, C) used under I are parts of
        topic I.
     4. If subdivisions are placed under A, B, C, they in turn
        are parts of the larger topic.
        (Example)
        I. High school departments
           A. Social sciences
              1. American history
              2. Civics
           B. Mathematics
              1. Algebra
              2. Geometry
                 a. plane
     5. All minor divisions are parts of the larger topic under
        which they are placed.

IV. There are several fundamental rules of outlining.
    A. Most speech outlines contain from two to four major divisions in the discussion of the body of the speech.
        1. A three- or four-minute speech rarely has more than three divisions and usually only two.
        2. The divisions are the main points of the speech that the speaker wishes the audience to remember.
        3. An audience can usually remember two or three central ideas; but they can't remember seven or eight.
        4. When too many points are mentioned, the speaker will not have the time to emphasize each point fully enough to make the audience remember it.
    A. The statements of each topic in an outline should be brief and concise.
    C. Each topic should represent a definite idea.
    D. The technique of making topic phrases from sentences can be used.
        1. Omit verbs.
        2. Express the idea of the verb in a noun formed from it.
        3. Begin topics with nouns preceded by adjectives.
        4. Important subsidiary ideas may be expressed as subtopics.
        5. Use a single word or a phrase of three or four words in a topic.
        6. Some examples of topic phrase making are as follows:
            a. "All over the world people are hoping that sometime we can find a peaceful method of settling our international disputes."
                (1) Simplify this idea.
                (2) Substitute: "Universal desire for peace."
            b. "Many men dislike the farm because of the long hours and the distance to the motion picture show."
                (1) Substitute: "Dislike of farm life."
                (2) "Use as subdivisions:
                    (a) long hours
                    (b) motion pictures
V. Summarize the outline.
    A. A carefully planned outline insures a speaker against a

rambling, uninteresting talk that does not accomplish any purpose except to tire the audience.
B. The outline gives the speaker a feeling of confidence and assurance.

INDEX